DETOX

FOR THE OVERLY RELIGIOUS //

DAVID PUTMAN

NASHVILLE, TENNESSEE

978-0-8054-4882-5

Published by B&H Publishing Group
Nashville, Tennessee

Dewey Decimal Classification: 248.84
Subject Heading: RELIGIOUS LIFE \ CHURCH WORK \
JESUS CHRIST

1 2 3 4 5 6 7 8 • 14 13 12 11 10

For Tami

Acknowledgments

This book is a reflection of my journey in losing my religion and rediscovering Jesus and his ways. A special thanks to . . .

- My wife Tami, I can't imagine doing life without you.
- My children Dave and Amanda, who are quick to call me out when I start getting religious and who insist I keep it real.
- My spiritual family and the ministry team at Mountain Lake Church, who continue to show me how to become less religious and more about Jesus.
- The young men of the 82nd Airborne, who have brought much life and joy into our home over this past year. I salute you and pray for your safe return.
- My Friend Beth Nelson, who has spent hours making sense out of my ramblings.
- The gang at B&H: Tom Walters, Kim Stanford, Jeff Godby, and Tim Jordon who has championed this book well.
- All who dare to take this journey

Contents

Book Three: Leaving What Jesus Leaves Behind

Getting Started

I want to invite you on a journey, a journey to rediscover the simplicity of Jesus.

Not long ago in a discussion with a group of young pastors, I was overwhelmed by the complexity the conversation took as we talked about Jesus and his ways. As I listened, I felt I was going to explode. Finally I spoke up, "Guys, it's not that complicated. Jesus and his ways are really simple. We have made it far too complex." I really believe this. I am convinced that Jesus is about simple. Religion has made following Jesus way too complex. And each of us must discover Jesus and the simplicity of Jesus for ourselves.

As I began this journey, I heard an ever so slight knocking at my heart's door. At first I didn't recognize it. Over time it became louder and louder until I couldn't deny it. To be completely honest, what really got my attention was a bomb. It was the bomb that blew up my son's Humvee while he served with the 82nd Airborne in Afghanistan. When you get a call that your son has been hit with a bomb and is on his way by helicopter to a military hospital somewhere in the middle of Afghanistan, it's amazing how loud the knocking gets. When you really need Jesus, you start looking for him. That's what I did. And that's when I heard this knocking and realized Jesus was on the other side of the door, seeking to gain reentry. The amazing thing was I didn't know he was on the outside of my life. I discovered that, over time, Jesus had gently been nudged out of my life by religion.

Opening the door again to Jesus has had a domino effect in my life. Domino after domino of previous religious thought and understanding has fallen. A whole new way of life has emerged. I am in the process of finding my way, but more importantly, finding Jesus and his way. I invite you to join me on this journey.

Why the Gospels?

Since this journey is about rediscovering the simplicity of Jesus and his ways, I've chosen to make it a focused journey. For the past year or so I have limited my reading in the Bible to the four Gospels: Matthew, Mark, Luke, and John. It's not that I don't think the other parts of Scripture are inspired. Matter of fact, as I've traveled this journey, my appetite for the Old Testament and the Epistles has greatly increased. I can't wait to break my strange kind of fast and jump back into the rest of God's story with both feet.

Back to the Gospels. Beginning in Matthew, I have read and reread the Gospels. Each time I have asked Jesus to show me his way.

I'm glad I did. It is now very difficult for me to miss Jesus in the Bible, no matter where I begin my reading. It's been an amazing journey, beginning with Jesus' words, "Repent, for the kingdom of heaven is near" (Matt. 4:17) and continuing the journey by watching his kingdom unfold.

Live, Love, and Leave

I've written this book in three major sections that follow my definition of what it means to be a follower of Jesus: someone who lives like Jesus, loves like Jesus, and leaves what Jesus left behind (others who live like Jesus and love like Jesus). I've resisted the temptation to try to connect all the dots, realizing my best journeys have often been spontaneous and erratic in nature. At the same time, you will find some order to my madness.

Read It Devotionally

I begin each chapter with the words of Jesus followed with two brief statements that contrast toxic religion with the Jesus way. This is designed to get you thinking, sometimes shock you, or rattle your cage a little. At the end of each chapter, you will find a few questions to ponder and a place where you can write down your thoughts and prayers, or doodle a little (doodling is an artistic expression when you can't find words to express the Jesus you've just encountered).

As you take this journey, realize that while our stories may be similar, they will be different, for they are our own unique stories. Jesus is writing his gospel in my life. His living gospel is also being written in your life. I can't wait to see what he has in store for all of us as our stories continue to unfold. Make sure you visit www.find ingthejesusway.com and let me know about your journey.

As you enter this journey, let me encourage you to use the words I have penned as a catalyst for your own journey. Like any journey, your journey will have a definite starting point. Maybe you have already begun that journey. I imagine you have. There will be times in the journey that you will traverse it with ease. There will be other times when the terrain of your experience will be littered with confusion, obstacles, and challenges. There will be other times that you will lose your way. Fear will cause you to want to retreat to what is most familiar. Faith, as your traveling companion, will lead you on. There will be times that we disagree along the journey. I think my wife and I disagreed last night. Guess what? We still love each other.

As you take this journey, don't get in a hurry. Remember, it's not the destiny as much as it is the journey with Jesus where you will experience the greatest excitement, fulfillment, adventure, and joy. I personally recommend that you read this book devotionally, a chapter every day or so, pausing to reflect, camping out occasionally, and even backtracking when needed. That's the way I wrote it.

I have spent much time reflecting on my own experiences and the Jesus I have encountered along the way. I have had good days and bad days. I have viewed the simplicity of Jesus and his ways from the mountaintop and from the valley. I have encountered the Evil One along the way with his discouraging taunts. You will too! But at the end of the day, it is my prayer that you might draw strength, encouragement, and comfort from Jesus as you journey. And then, if somehow this book helps you discover the simplicity of Jesus and his ways, my mission will be accomplished.

Warning: Detox Needed!

It would serve us well to reflect on the words of Jesus, our counselor and comforter, "The thief comes only to steal and kill and destroy; I have come that they may have life, and have it to the full" (John 10:10). Satan doesn't want us to live like Jesus or love like Jesus, and he certainly doesn't want us to leave what Jesus left behind. While Jesus came inviting us into his way in order that we might experience a full life, Satan wants to limit and minimize our lives; he often does this by introducing us to cheap substitutes like religion. The substitute is that which ever so subtly nudges Jesus out of our lives. Over time we replace our relationship "with Jesus" with a religion "about Jesus." We become blind to his truth and numb to his presence.

When this happens, detoxing is required. Detoxing is a slow process that requires help along the way. We were never meant to journey alone. We all have had to encounter or deal with addiction. Those of us who have to deal with it firsthand seldom see our need for detoxing, on our own. When confronted with our need, we often find ourselves denying it. Maybe you're confronting it right now! When we at first embrace the need to detox, we often choose to do it alone. This seldom works. Often detoxing requires an intervention. Those of us who need detoxing find ourselves bartering and bargaining with others. All the while arguing that we can do it on our own. This seldom happens. Detoxing requires going through it with others. We need others to give us permission and perspective, hold us accountable, and encourage us. Other times we simply need someone to hold us as we face the pain of giving up the old and embracing the new. The same is true of detoxing from religion. We need each other. We all lose our way and together we can best find our way back to Jesus and his ways.

As you read this book, don't do it alone. Go through it with a small group of people who share your desire to rediscover the simplicity of Jesus and his ways. If not a small group, pick one or two fellow travelers who can relate to where you are. Jesus promises us that where two or three are gathered he will be in our midst. WARNING! Those who join you on the journey must be ready, or they will hold you back and make it difficult to experience progress. Pause and pray for God to guide you to whom you should share this journey with. Now listen! What do you hear him saying? Pay close attention to whom you encounter or think of today.

Take your time as you begin this journey, for healing happens best over time. Also, understand that the truth Jesus is about to bring into your life will be healing. At the same time, the truth that heals is often the truth that hurts. More important, remember that Jesus is the Great Physician and he is inviting us into his way. He desires to bring spiritual healing into our lives. He even promises to take the journey with us, never leaving us alone. He goes as far as to give us his Spirit as our ultimate guide. Listen closely as he leads on this journey. Expect him to speak to you in a new way. Expect him to change your life. Expect it to happen over time. Expect to meet a new you along the way. That's what he is doing for me!

BOOK ONE

Living Like Jesus Lives

Jesus is our life, and his life can be experienced only when we decrease and allow him to increase. This was the very prayer of John the Baptist, the same John that Jesus spoke these words about: "I tell you the truth: Among those born of women there has not risen anyone greater" (Matt. 11:11). A little less of me and a little more of Jesus each day is the Jesus way. This is what it means to live like Jesus. A lifetime spent living like Jesus is a lifetime well spent.

CHAPTER 1

Simplicity . . . A Means to an End

"Come to me, all you who are weary and burdened,
and I will give you rest."

—Matthew 11:28

Toxic Religion: I have to live up to a certain standard in order to be accepted by God.

The Jesus Way: As I place my trust in Jesus, God completely accepts me into his presence and family no matter what.

Not very long ago I noticed tension between Jesus' ways and the way I was living my life. I was in the middle of writing a book on what it means to live like Jesus, love like Jesus, and leave what Jesus left behind (which is those who live like him and love like him). As I found myself reading and rereading the Gospels, I became captivated by the simplicity of the way he lived and loved. Overwhelmed, I realized that my life and my relationship with him had become way too complicated and were going to require a major overhaul.

It's not that I had fallen off the wagon, committed some big sin, had a midlife crisis (I did buy a motorcycle), or even gone through a major life change. I realized, however, that over time my life had become inundated with complexities. My thoughts were filled with complicated explanations of faith, my relationships were knotted and mangled, my daily schedule was beyond hectic, my expressions of love took on a contrived tone, my personal habits and disciplines were heaped with exacting precision, my church life was filled with the orchestration of details and plans, and my approaches to discipleship were demanding and exhausting. In short, just about everything I did was the product of complexity. With this complexity came a kind of exhaustion I had become far too familiar with. I think most of us know this kind of dragging, oppressive exhaustion. If you doubt it, start counting the number of times in a given day a friend tells you he's tired. Even better, count how many times in a day *you* tell someone that *you* are tired.

The Jesus Way

As I read and reread the Gospels, it became more and more apparent to me that the Jesus I found there was extraordinarily simple. What's more, he invites us into a relationship of simplicity: "Come to me, all you who are weary and burdened, and I will give you rest. Take my yoke upon you and learn from me, for I am gentle and humble in heart, and you will find rest for your souls. For my yoke is easy and my burden is light" (Matt. 11:28–30).

Jesus knew we would face the temptation to complicate our lives with religion. He knew we would be inclined to put limits and demands on ourselves that would slowly, subtly bring us to a breaking point. In fact, it was already happening even in Jesus' time.

Jesus was a rabbi, and as a teacher one of his primary responsibilities was to interpret the Torah (the first five books of the Bible) for his followers. The Torah is the holiest of Scriptures to the Jews, and included within it are the Ten Commandments as well as 613 additional laws about worship, cleanliness, marriage, nutrition, and every other aspect of Jewish life. Any given rabbi's interpretation of the Torah consisted of dozens of *hedges*, which were additional oral laws or rules designed to protect the Law (this includes the extra 613). A rabbi would have had thousands of little laws or hedges he taught as his interpretation of the Torah, his suggested way of living. This way of living was referred to as that rabbi's *yoke*, and every rabbi had a distinctive yoke.

When you consider this context, Jesus' call to "come to me, all you who are weary and burdened, and I will give you rest" takes on new significance. Jesus was addressing those burdened by the impossible weight of the religion of that day. Jewish law was immense in itself, yet the Hebrew people had to follow not only the biblical law but also the extraneous yoke of their rabbi of choice. Jesus invites his followers into a new way, a way to enter into his life. He promises us that he is gentle, humble in heart, and that we will find rest from the complexities of our hedged-up religions. Remarkably, the yoke Jesus offers doesn't add weight to our shoulders; it removes it. The rest we gain from following his way begins with taking his yoke on us—his way of life. He promises us that his yoke is different: it is easy and it is light.

Anything Can Become Religion

Jesus invites us who are weary and burdened by religion to take his yoke upon us. He understood that the religion of the Pharisees left the people miserable. Any parameters we place on our relationship with Jesus, anything that becomes "law" in our lives, is religion. For example, having a daily time with God is a common practice and discipline for those who follow Jesus. It is a good thing. It allows us to refocus and re-center our lives on Jesus. When I spend regular time with Jesus—reading his word, listening to him, capturing my thoughts about him (journaling), and talking to him—I experience his intimacy. If I am to follow him, I have to have theses times of closeness. However, if our lives become more about our daily routine, something we check off (I've done my quiet time or had my daily appointment with God), then the Jesus we encounter during that special time becomes a law that we hedge ourselves in. When this happens, our relationship with him becomes more about religious activity we have to do in order to be right or accepted.

To be really honest with you, I have discovered the more disciplined, compartmentalized, and rigid I have become with my early morning quiet time, the less I experience Jesus in my daily walk. As a pastor I often move from task list to task list, checking off each religious activity with zeal. It becomes more about the doing and less about the being.

On the other hand, it is a beautiful thing when I get in rhythm with Jesus. Often I wake up early in the morning and I feel his closeness and it draws me into worship. I find myself sitting before him, reflecting on his goodness, reading his gospel, journaling my thoughts, confessing my sin, praying for a friend, having my heart filled with his love and expanded for others. Other times I get up and I feel his gentle nudge to begin writing about his thoughts that he has placed in my heart sometime and somehow during my sleep. There are other times I hear him tell me to sit near my wife as she prepares for her day and serve as a conduit of his love for her. Regular time is important with God, but it's not the end, only the beginning. When my relationship is less rigid and more spontaneous, it is not unusual for him to interrupt my day with his closeness and his agenda. Recently in our regular weekly meeting with a friend, God spoke to us, inviting us into a time of prayer that quickly turned into worship. It was so humbling and renewing.

You can see how it doesn't take long for religion to take a downward turn. It quickly becomes about something we do or don't do in order to meet the expectations or approval of God and others. It can consist of rituals, practices, or even spiritual disciplines that we begin to substitute for our relationship with Jesus. It could be a certain way of praying, attending the right church, giving an amount of money to a charitable cause, ascribing to a set of doctrines, or serving to such an extent that the action begins to overtake the intent. All of these things can be good, but they can also become a substitute for an intimate relationship with God. When this happens, we become religious. And when we become religious, our lives become complicated.

Religion can also be defined by the things we don't do. I grew up in the South, where we lived by the mantra, "Don't smoke, drink, curse, chew, or dance with girls that do." You probably had similar restrictions on your adolescence, and you may have even carried them into adulthood. These, too, are the markings of a religious life. We become so concerned with not doing the wrong thing that we ignore our subtle wandering into pride, greed, jealousy, and other less overt offenses. We become defined by what we are against instead of what we are for or, more importantly, *whom* we are for.

It's no wonder we're tired. We forbid ourselves from doing one thing, while requiring ourselves to do others—all superfluously. I began to understand this when I realized that my entire life was tired. My thoughts, my relationships, my schedule, my marriage, my habits, my job, and even my free time had become tired. I had placed so many laws on myself, so much religion, that I became unable to function normally. Think of an animal: When a horse has too heavy a load on its back, it's unable to walk even the straightest, easiest trail because it can't manage its load. This is what I had done to myself. This is what we have all done to ourselves.

Beware Lest We Add Hedges Unaware

We can't blame ourselves entirely though. These yokes of religion are being laid upon us constantly by a variety of sources. We may live this way because it's all we know, but it's possible that someone or some group of people gave us this yoke. A church or pastor may have placed this load on your shoulders, directly or indirectly, intentionally or inadvertently. Chances are someone communicated that in order to be right, to be fulfilled, to have purpose, to be accepted, or to get God's approval, you had to live up to a standard, probably a very high one. And a wall has been built around you, with row after row of laws and hedges and more laws and more hedges, such that you are unable to see over it anymore, to see into the quiet, beautiful simplicity of Jesus and his ways.

Whether you built your own hedge or it was given to you, the truth is that we can never do enough to get God's approval, and we can certainly never do enough to meet everyone else's approval. What great news that God accepts us just as we are and invites us into a relationship based on his love and his love alone!

Detox Isn't Easy

At the same time, why do I feel better about myself when I am doing all these things? Even when I'm exhausted, why is it that I can't stop continuing to strive to meet these expectations and requirements? I see it all the time. Today there's a new tribe of churches emerging that are going simple. Thom Rainer and Eric Geiger brought this to our attention in *Simple Church*. Simple churches need simple followers. The church where I serve, Mountain Lake Church, would be considered a simple church, and I often watch those coming from more complex churches try to make the transition. They are overwhelmed by the simplicity. They often become restless wanting more to do. Their questions about our programming are often slanted toward activities that allow them to consume. Many of them don't make the journey and opt to return to the complexities of their old ways. This is why we need to submit ourselves to an intensive religion detox.

Embracing the simplicity of Jesus not only involves learning, it involves unlearning and relearning. No one who has ever experienced a detoxification process would call it easy—there's a lot to contend with like withdrawal, formation of new habits, new relationships, and the sense of loss that comes with giving up the old. Jesus invited Nicodemus to leave the old and embrace the new when he said: "I tell you the truth, no one can see the kingdom of God unless he is born again" (John 3:3). Old behaviors and patterns have to be put to rest. We must be born again from our religion, from our self-imposed yokes, from the weight of our burdens. It isn't easy, but the result is a chance to break free from the weight we have borne and live in the freedom and simplicity of Jesus.

A Whole New Life Awaits You

Recently I was talking with my wife, Tami, about our journey. She said something that really grabbed my attention, "I never thought it could be this way." She talked about how Jesus had invited us out of the weight of our sin and into his way, but somehow over time we had become religious. Our lives were more defined by what we did and didn't do than by our relationship with Jesus. Maybe you can relate. She talked about the freedom we are now experiencing, following Jesus and his ways. What an affirmation as I write this book. I pray that you reach the same conclusion as you make your way through this book, but more importantly that you will come to discover what it means to simply follow him.

We must ultimately understand that life is a journey, and life change is an ongoing part of this journey. Only God can change the heart and liberate the soul. However, imagine for a moment if you could really discover the simplicity of Jesus and his ways. Imagine a new way of living that begins and ends each day with following Jesus, free of condemnation.

Jesus described his yoke as "easy" and his burden as "light." I believe his invitation is for all of us, and I am living this for the first time in my life. Imagine for a moment a simple life, a life in which you don't have to live up and you don't have to live down. Imagine if you didn't have to lead. All you had to do is simply follow Jesus. Imagine a life lived out of the overflow of an intimate relationship with him. Imagine a life in which you are accepted just as you are.

This is possible when we lose our religion and discover or rediscover the simplicity of the Jesus way.

DAY 1: FINDING THE JESUS WAY

1. Describe how religion creeps into your life and robs you of your relationship with Jesus.
2. What steps do you need to take to rediscover the simplicity of Jesus?
3. What are the hedges in your own life that you need to cut down?
4. What does detoxing look like for you?
5. Name two or three people you can share this journey with.

Thoughts, Prayers, and Doodles on the Jesus Way

_____

_____

_____

_____

_____

_____

_____

_____

_____

_____

_____

CHAPTER 2

Rethink . . . What If I'm Wrong?

> *"Repent, for the kingdom of heaven is near."*
> —Matthew 4:17

Toxic Religion: I have to be right all the time in order to be right with God.

The Jesus Way: It's not about being right or wrong, but about being in relationship with Jesus and others in the context of grace.

What if I'm wrong? That's right, what if I'm wrong when it comes to my understanding of Jesus and his ways?

For the past few decades, I have defined what it means to be a follower of Jesus through my own egocentric lens. This lens is my worldview. For the most part I adopted and adapted this view from the Western church. I thought that being a follower of Jesus was all about my salvation, my purity, my quiet time, my personal mission, my peace. Me. My. And while there isn't anything wrong with my salvation, my purity, my quiet time, my personal mission, and my peace, that's certainly not the complete story of the gospel. When Jesus invited us to come follow him, he had so much more in mind than simply fueling our consumptive nature with religion. Jesus never intended for us to consume him like an energy drink, in search of a little spiritual pick-me-up.

Following Jesus Begins with Rethinking

As I read and reread the Gospels, I am stopped in my tracks by the words with which Jesus kicked off his earthly ministry: "Repent, for the kingdom of heaven is near." Jesus began his public ministry with the word *repent*. You talk about a radical way to begin. As a pastor I can think of only one time in my entire ministry that I began a sermon with "repent."

The church I was pastoring had lost its way, and I knew I had to get the people's attention. All week I prayed about what God would have me do and say. On that Sunday morning I asked our leaders to meet with me. I told them we weren't going to do business as usual that day. Without any music or any of the programming that usually went with our weekend services, I entered the worship auditorium and went directly to the podium. I began the service that day with a message of repentance. I called them out, pointing to one religious behavior after another. That day I functioned as a prophet. I approached it with humility. I had prayed and wept for the people all week. At first the congregation was shocked, but soon the message began to hit home. God did a fresh work in our lives that day. He brought a divided people together as one. He recaptured our hearts and devotion. It was an amazing day.

Jesus began his ministry in a similar way by telling us to rethink, to do a 180 and turn from everything. He invited us into a whole new way of life that turns everything upside down, a way of life that includes changing the way we think about our egocentrism, our sins, our failed relationships, our pride, our limited vision, and our mixed-up religious ways.

Heaven on Earth

With this in mind, I have been asking myself a lot of questions about everything I have believed and how I have lived out my faith, profession, belief, confession, or whatever you want to call it. I'm now more convinced than ever that I have been wrong. I always thought the Christian life was about my going to heaven and taking as many people with me as possible. What if there is more to following Jesus than simply me being good and going to heaven? That's what I'm discovering. I'm beginning to understand that I was wrong, not about everything, but about many things. There is so much more to Jesus and his ways. He wants me—and all of us—to be part of bringing heaven to earth. That's right, heaven! Right here, right now. In response (this is where the repenting comes in), I'm working to abandon my self-centered nature and allowing him to retread my life in order that I might learn to follow him and his ways. It's one thing to live for the future, anticipating his kingdom to come one day. It's another thing to live in the moment, realizing that his kingdom is coming right now and that I get to participate in it every moment of my life. I'm discovering that living in his kingdom requires a lot of rethinking, repenting, and ultimately reliving on my part. It is a whole new way of living.

This repentance involves a rethinking of everything I thought I knew about heaven. I always thought the minute you invited Jesus into your life, you received a little bit of heaven right then. I would have even said that heaven begins the moment you become a follower of Jesus. But since I began this process of repenting by reading and rereading the Gospels, something is happening to me. I feel like I am being born again as I awaken to the kingdom of heaven each day. I am discovering that there is not a little of heaven here right now, but there is a whole lot of heaven right here and Jesus wants more of heaven here.

Religion Nudges Jesus Out

It's easy to see how you can become toxically religious when you think following Jesus is all about you. That's exactly what happened with me. It happened slowly, but over a lifetime of following Jesus, little by little Jesus had been nudged out of the center of my life. I realized he had been replaced by something akin to shallow morality.

Back to that picture of Jesus I spoke about in "Getting Started": "Here I am! I [Jesus] stand at the door and knock. If anyone hears my voice and opens the door, I will come in and eat with him, and he with me" (Rev. 3:20). As I read the Gospels in light of the kingdom of heaven being at hand, I began to hear a subtle knocking. At first I didn't recognize where it came from, but over time the knocking became clearer. It was Jesus, and he was outside my life trying to get in.

Upon closer examination, I realized he wasn't just outside my life—he is outside our churches. Why can't we who are inside hear him? And why won't we just open the door? I think I know why! Religion has a way of drowning out the heartbeat of Jesus. Ultimately we must confront the realization that this could well be a picture of our lives: Jesus, on the outside of our lives and our churches, even entire denominations or networks, asking gently to be allowed in.

Recently I was waiting to be seated in a restaurant. A group ahead of us appeared to be family and friends. They were having a great time together; it was the holidays and they were celebrating while they waited to be seated. I'm not sure how it happened, but one of their young daughters slipped out of the restaurant. They didn't see her leave, and no one else did either. When her family and friends discovered she had left, they were startled. I could hear them say, "How did she get outside? Why was she out there?" One of them— I think it was her mother—ran out the door and brought her back in a few minutes, clenched to her bosom.

Likewise, somehow Jesus has been nudged out of our churches in the midst of our celebrating. First, we must realize he is no longer on the inside. We must let Jesus back in. We must open the door and let him inside. And letting him in requires repentance.

Competing Views

Letting Jesus in is a dangerous proposition. It requires relooking, rethinking, reorienting, and retreading our lives for kingdom living. When Jesus began his public ministry, he entered a highly religious world of competing kingdom views. The Jews were under the oppressive iron rule of the Romans. Anticipation of a Messiah was at a fever pitch. There were several political parties in Israel at the time, and each of them had their own take on what this Messiah would be like, what they must do to prepare the way for him, and what his kingdom would be like once it came.

When you examine these political parties, it's easy to see why Jesus began his ministry with "repent." Each group's ideology had backfired. Instead of preparing the way for the Messiah, they had paved a way that had inadvertently nudged him out of the picture. In many ways we do the same thing; I can see a lot of myself in all these different parties. Perhaps you can as well. Unfortunately this leads to a kind of religious cocktail that impacts our understanding of Jesus and his kingdom. No wonder Jesus came out of his corner of heaven swinging the "repent" word. Let's take a closer look by examining what these political parties brought to the table.

Moralism

There is certainly nothing wrong with morality. I think we would all agree that a little more morality would be a good thing in our world. The Pharisees certainly felt this way. This explains their relentless religious natures. This explains their oral law and the thousands and thousands of hedges they erected in around the Law to protect and ensure that the Law was lived out. The Pharisees really believed the way to prepare for the Messiah was through moral purity. Rid the world of sex, drugs, and rock and roll, and then the Messiah would come, kicking Rome's backside. Perhaps this is the party I most identify with from my religious background and upbringing. For most of my life I have focused my religious energy on moralism. And when moralism becomes our reason for living, we become most like the Pharisees.

At the same time Jesus didn't come to abolish the Old Testament Law but to fulfill its demands, setting us free to live in his power and presence. He goes on to tell us that he didn't come for the righteous but the sinner. Moralistic religion doesn't need Jesus. Moralists are good enough, or at least so busy being good enough that they miss this new righteousness. Jesus is our righteousness. When we realize this, it frees us to live the Jesus way.

Separatism

Out of the Pharisees came an even more extreme religious party, the Essenes. The Essenes were known for their separatism. They lived celibate and communal lives outside the cities. They formed their own suburban utopia—monastic communities where they waited for the Messiah to come take them to heaven. They had no contact with the outside world. They separated themselves from the pagans of the day. They took the idea of being in the world but not of the world to an extreme, and they checked out. They accomplished this by creating religious compounds for believers that bear a strong resemblance to some of our churches today. Sound familiar?

Many of us today choose this brand of religion. We have churches for members only. We have schools designed to keep our kids safe from any thought that might challenge the gospel or at least our view of it. We have our religious broadcast networks designed to keep us safe from the media of today's world. The list goes on and on. We believe that Jesus will come one day and take us out of this evil world. In the meantime, we spend all our energy and effort creating religious hedges. The Jesus way leads us to a whole new way of life. We come to understand that in Jesus we are set free to go into the world to show others the Jesus way. It's hard to go into the world when we are content hiding in the comfort of our religious compounds.

Syncretism

The Sadducees were known for their alliance with the Romans. They lived in the here and now. They didn't believe in the resurrection or the new life that God offers those who embrace the Jesus way. They would say they really didn't have it so bad here on earth. They believed the center of religious life was the temple and the Law. Leave the Romans alone and pay the Roman taxes and they will leave us alone. It was a sort of blend-in-and-don't-rock-the-boat mentality.

The syncretics weren't the only party with this mind-set. The Herodians enjoyed a close relationship with Herod the Great and were alleged by the early Christian Tertullian to consider him a messiah.[1] Regardless of their motives, both parties agreed that the best solution was adopting a policy of relevance in which their culture blended easily with Rome. In our Western church world we face a very similar relativism. As you can imagine, Jesus was a threat to this kind of behavior. He still is today.

Activism

Finally there were the Zealots. They believed the answer was an open rebellion against the ruling power. They agreed that the reason they were in the shape they were in was because they did not stand up against the evil empire of the Romans. In standing up against Rome, they believed God would give them victory. God was on their side, and the way to see his kingdom come was with a sword. This group was quick to march, protest, and invoke an "eye for an eye." If they existed today, they would be quick to bomb abortion clinics and boycott movies, businesses, and theme parks. Taken to an extreme, they would be the ones most likely to strap bombs to their bodies or turn their vehicles into weapons as they lash out against the evil Western empire.

This is the volatile religious and political world that Jesus entered. It is as if Jesus is saying, "Hold it, stop everything! You are all wrong. I'm going to show you a whole new way. This new way is my way. Come, follow me, for the kingdom of heaven is near."

A New Set of Lenses

Jesus came inviting all to repent and enter his kingdom. This kingdom was and still is radically different from the little kingdoms we set up as cheap substitutes. When Jesus appeared on the scene of his day, his message was intended largely for this religiously charged community.

As I reflect on the Jesus of the Gospels, I'm coming to realize that Jesus' message is for me. Out of all these groups, I most closely identify with the Pharisees, but I'm certain I have a little of the others in me as well. I have always felt it was my responsibility to live a good moral life. I still do. I've attended church, given my tithes and offerings, kept a daily quiet time, been faithful to my wife, stayed away from alcohol, generally been a good citizen, mostly voted for traditional conservative issues, and been a good Christian. Yet Jesus warned us in Matthew 5:20, "For I tell you that unless your righteousness surpasses that of the Pharisees and the teachers of the law, you will certainly not enter the kingdom of heaven." The Pharisees made it their jobs to be perfect, even coming up with their own standards or at least their interpretation of standards. For Jesus "righteousness" was about justice and Jesus taught that his justice had to do with the proper use of power, not some moral code that can be lived out in our own power. How can my righteousness possibly surpass that of the Pharisees?

In rethinking my religion through the lens of Jesus' radical message, I notice that he didn't specifically tell the Pharisees to repent, nor did he point his finger at the "sinners." He simply said for everyone to hear, "Repent, for the kingdom of heaven is near" (Matt. 4:17). This single word is for all of us. It has been said that the ground is level at the cross, so the message is the same to all: Repent and follow Jesus.

Repentance isn't easy, but it is supremely rewarding. I don't feel overwhelmed, condemned, frustrated, threatened, unaccepted, depressed, or inadequate. I feel more alive and free than I ever have. Jesus' words ring true in my life: "I have come that they may have life, and have it to the full" (John 10:10). I am on a journey, and for the first time in a long time I am beginning to experience a fullness that comes from Jesus alone.

Your experience with repentance may have involved a state of brokenness. It still does, but that is only a small part of it. Jesus didn't tell us to make our lives miserable by beating ourselves up; instead he told us, "The time has come. The kingdom of God is near. Repent and believe the good news!" (Mark 1:15). Jesus' idea of repentance is more about entering into a new relationship with him, taking on a new yoke, and embracing a new way—his way.

The thing about repentance is that you can't merely turn around and stop. You can't turn your back on your old ways and congratulate yourself on a job well done. Repentance requires you to begin walking in the *opposite* direction. It is a never-ending process. It is a way of life. You don't arrive at repentance; you start there. You may find yourself, as I have, slipping back into old beliefs and behaviors, but you have to keep moving forward, rethinking and relearning over and over again the simple way of Jesus. With every repentant step, you must embrace your humanity, God's love for you, and his invitation into Jesus' way.

Living like Jesus will present a whole new array of challenges. Living like Jesus puts the spotlight on my innermost thoughts and motivations. Living like Jesus pushes me out of comfort and forces me to give up the toxic religion I have knowingly and unknowingly used to control my circumstances. Living like Jesus nudges me forward to a place where I can see the world and its inhabitants in a whole new light. The way of living that ushers in Jesus' kingdom is here.

The time is right now. The kingdom is right here. The invitation is clear. Rethink! And know there is more good news to come;— Jesus is breaking out his kingdom through us. His kingdom comes when we let Jesus live through us, changing what we do, say, and live from the inside out.

DAY 2: FINDING THE JESUS WAY

1. What is the difference between living as if heaven is somewhere out there and living as if heaven is right here, right now?
2. What does "rethinking" look like for you?
3. What areas of your life do you need to rethink, let go, and hand over to Jesus?
4. What does righteousness look like in your life?

Thoughts, Prayers, and Doodles on the Jesus Way

CHAPTER 3

Come . . . Just as You Are

"Come, follow me . . . and I will make you fishers of men."
—Matthew 4:19

> **Toxic Religion:** We invite Jesus into our lives, to meet our needs.
>
> **The Jesus Way:** Jesus invites us into his life to follow him on a journey that involves a lifetime.

For months I had been praying for one thing, and I didn't even realize it. Looking back over my journal, I was surprised to see I had written this prayer almost daily. It was on my pen and in my heart: *Show me your way.*

I had been operating out of a paradigm that invited Jesus into my life; now for the first time, I realized that Jesus was inviting me into *his* life, into his way. I hadn't heard this invitation from him because I had been too busy insisting that he come into my life. While reading and rereading the Gospels, I began to see a pattern:

Jesus always does the inviting. He is constantly extending his invitation for us to follow him.

There is nothing wrong with inviting Jesus into our lives. Jesus must be invited into our lives, but it doesn't end there. Inviting him into our lives is where our lives end and his life in us begins.

The Jesus way begins with Jesus. We invite him into our lives in order that we might follow him. He gives us his Spirit. He becomes our companion. He becomes our leader and forgiver. Then, we follow. At that point, we must surrender control and begin to let him have his way in our lives. Our prayer changes from *Jesus, come into my life* to *Jesus, show me your way*. Learning to respond to this new way of praying sets us up for a life of following him and his ways.

Summons by the Chief and Elders

I was reminded of this on a recent trip to Africa. We had come to Malawi to build a well and irrigation system in a village, and after two weeks we were wrapping up our project. The village chief had been a key part of the whole undertaking, and his presence and hospitality signaled to the rest of the village that he was in full support. I asked him to gather the village at high noon on our last day (an archaic substitute for my iPhone clock) so we could dedicate the well. I arrived midmorning to find the hillside filled with the people of the village. The mood was electric. The chief and I climbed a small mound of dirt that served as our makeshift podium, and together we addressed the village.

After the chief spoke to the people, I told him I would like to talk to them about Jesus and his ways, and the chief agreed. I spoke about how the water provided by the well would change their lives. I told them the water could be used to wash the dirt and grime from their bodies (because of a scarcity of water, personal hygiene was a luxury), but Jesus spoke of water that cleans us from the inside out. I spoke about how the water could quench their thirst, but that Jesus spoke of water that could quench the thirst in their souls. I went on to tell them that Jesus was that water, and he wanted them to drink from his perfect and unending supply. I invited the people, clearly and simply, to drink from Jesus' well of life. I asked them to stand if they wanted to come follow Jesus.

They looked at me, unmoving. After a few awkward moments, I did what any preacher would do in a tight spot: I prayed and then dismissed them.

As the people dispersed, our interpreter came and told me the chief wanted to speak with me. I wasn't sure what he wanted, but I knew the village was home to a very dark, traditional African religion. Maybe I had gone too far.

As I approached the chief, I noticed that the village elders were with him. I wasn't sure if that was a good sign or not. The chief immediately began to speak, and when my interpreter relayed the chief's words, I couldn't believe my ears. The chief said, "The words you spoke about Jesus have warmed my heart. I want to know more about this Jesus and his ways." I told the chief that we had all lost our way and that Jesus had come to show us a new way. I explained as well as I could about his death and resurrection for our sin. I told the chief that Jesus wants us all to live in his kingdom and that this begins with inviting Jesus into our lives. I asked if he would like to invite Jesus into his life, and he did. Right there under the tree by our water project, the chief and his elders prayed a prayer inviting Jesus into their lives.

I was overwhelmed by what I had experienced but I wondered if inviting Jesus is just the beginning, how would the chief learn to follow Jesus? How would he come to know Jesus more intimately? How would the chief come to understand his ways? Who would help the chief understand Jesus' work in him through the Spirit? I knew the threat that the chief would never come to understand this new relationship without prompting. I asked my interpreter if we could get Bibles for the chief and his elders, and he assured me that not only would he bring them all Bibles, he would come back and begin teaching the chief about Jesus and showing him Jesus' ways. Our interpreter knew Jesus, and he knew that inviting Jesus into his life was the first step toward following.

Follow Me

The other day I received an e-mail from the interpreter. It was good news: He was spending the weekend with the chief. The chief had welcomed the interpreter into his home and was learning about Jesus firsthand. I was blown away. With this news I am assured that the chief is coming to understand what it means to follow Jesus. I can't wait to return to Africa and see my new friend and brother.

Imagine that you were the chief: upon hearing the gospel for the first time, how would you get to know Jesus and learn about his ways? Is there a verse or passage you might choose above the rest? Perhaps you would look to the first disciples, the ones Jesus called immediately after beginning his earthly ministry. Throwing their nets over the sides of their fishing boats, they jumped at the opportunity to answer his call: "Come, follow me . . . and I will make you fishers of men" (Matt. 4:19).

Notice the simplicity of Jesus' instructions to Peter and Andrew: "Come, follow me." That's it. No prayer. No ritual. No eighteen-month small-group commitment. No completing an attendance form. "Just follow me. Go where I go. Do what I do. Listen to what I say. Follow me." Jesus invited Peter and Andrew (and immediately afterward, James and John) into a relationship that would ultimately introduce them to a whole new way of life—his way. Jesus was inviting them to follow him. His invitation was to come and do life together.

The problem with inviting Jesus into our lives is we think we are the ones in control, the ones dictating the journey. We set the standard about what we want Jesus involved in and what we don't want him involved in. This is the opposite of what Jesus teaches us about his way. Jesus is the leader and he is inviting us to follow him, not the other way around. He calls the shots. He sets the pace. He leads the way. We simply follow.

Is He a Believer?

This idea came together for me on the way home from Africa. One of my traveling companions asked if someone we both knew was a believer. I responded, "He is a believer, but he's not following Jesus." He's not living the Jesus way. Many people believe but don't follow—it's a common practice in our religious world, in our Western world, and in our churches. There is a huge difference between believing and following. We live in a culture where everybody believes, but it's not enough to simply believe. Sure, believing can be a beginning point, but it certainly isn't the ending point. Jesus' invitation is to "come, follow me." He couldn't be more direct.

The disciples heard Jesus' call and dropped their nets. Perhaps it was easier for them than it is for us. They had heard stories of Jesus and were astounded by the idea that he was calling them by name, suggesting they come along with him. Be assured, however, that they were not looking for a religion. They had seen how the Pharisees and religious leaders of their day lived and wanted nothing to do with that type of religion. But in Jesus, they saw a personality, a sense of humor, a kindness, a compassion, a strength, a person, a new way of living that attracted them.

For these men to be invited to follow a rabbi was nothing short of a miracle. In their day, rabbis chose their disciples carefully, selecting the most promising Jewish boys to follow them, learn their ways, and maybe one day become rabbis themselves. They had been passed over by other teachers in favor of students with better families, more money, more promise, or a stronger education. Men like Peter,

Andrew, James, and John were quickly sorted out and sent home to apprentice in a trade with their fathers. These men became fishermen. Perhaps this explains why they left their nets so quickly at Jesus' simple invitation.

Jesus doesn't pick and choose the best. No, he invites all to come follow him. See how he reframes the religious paradigm of the day. No one is barred. Women, children, sinners, priests, all are invited to follow him.

Likewise, Jesus extends the same invitation to you and me. Even though others pass us by, he never does. He sees promise and potential in all of us, in even the most unlikely people, often choosing to use the weak and foolish over the strong and wise. It's no wonder the writings of Matthew, Mark, Luke, and John are referred to as the Good News—Jesus' invitation to come, follow him is good news to all.

Come as You Are

Jesus didn't say, "Clean up your life first, and then you can come." He simply said, "Come." The God of the universe invites us to come as we are. Peter, Andrew, James, and John were grime-under-their-fingernails, stinky-fish-smelling, grubby-clothes-wearing dirty. And Jesus couldn't have been more excited to have them join his band of disciples. Jesus saw in them a willingness to follow and a desire and an ability to be more. They knew their only chance of becoming like him was to follow him. The same thing is true for us. If we are to truly become like Jesus and embrace the simplicity of his ways, there is only one way to do it: Stop what you're doing, drop everything, and follow him.

Therefore, it is important that we define what it means to be a follower of Jesus. Following Jesus doesn't just mean believing in him—Jesus' own disciple (James) understood this when he said much later, "even the demons believe" (James 2:19). Following Jesus is about living like Jesus, loving like Jesus, and leaving what Jesus left behind (which is more people who live like him and love like him). That's what this book is about.

We hear, we understand, we follow, or maybe it's more like we hear, we follow, and then we understand. We reconsider our old ways in light of his invitation to follow. We repent, turning away from the toxic extras we've built and turning toward him and his way. We unlearn the habits, thoughts, and desires we once had and begin to form new habits, new thoughts, and new desires, new relationships that lead us down the path that follows Jesus.

Following him is a whole new way of life for many of us that involves a simple prayer: *Show me your way; I want to follow you.* As we pray this prayer or a similar one daily, we begin to see the kingdom of heaven coming in full bloom. We discover that Jesus is alive, he is relating to his world, and his kingdom is indeed coming. As we learn to follow him, we hear his voice, and out of the intimacy of our relationship we follow . . . we obey.

It's not as hard as we make it out to be. When we drop our religion and embrace Jesus and his ways, a whole new world opens up to us. This world involves entering his kingdom, and it's closer than we think.

DAY 3: FINDING THE JESUS WAY

1. What is the difference between "believing in Jesus" and "following Jesus"?
2. Jesus invites us to come. What does that mean for you?
3. Who can you share this amazing news with? Ask God to open up his way to you, giving you the courage to follow. Share this good news with someone.

Thoughts, Prayers, and Doodles on the Jesus Way

_____

_____

_____

_____

_____

_____

_____

_____

_____

_____

CHAPTER 4

Seeing . . . I Think I Have Something in My Eye

"Though seeing, they do not see; though hearing,
they do not hear or understand."

—Matthew 13:13

Toxic Religion: We are so busy with our religion we fail to see God at work in our world.

The Jesus Way: When we walk with Jesus, our eyes are opened to a whole new world that involves his kingdom coming on earth right now!

ould we be blinded by our own religion? Is God at work all around us and could we be so caught up in our religious framework that we can't see him? That's actually what Jesus said would happen: "Though seeing, they do not see; though hearing, they do not hear or understand." There is far more going on around us than we realize. Religion blinds us to seeing Jesus and his ways.

A few years ago my wife, Tami, was hit by a car while jogging in our neighborhood. Her leg was shattered, and she was immobilized for months. Each time I rounded the corner where the accident took place, I became angry. With each day and each trip past that corner, my anger grew until finally it came out. I just exploded. I walked upstairs where Tami was recovering on the couch, and I couldn't hold it in any longer.

"Tami, I'm so angry I don't know what to do. Every time I drive past that spot I get more and more furious."

Speaking very softly, she asked, "What are you angry about?"

"You!" I snapped. "I'm angry about you! Look what happened to you!"

Firmly, but still softly, she replied, "David, can't you see? Can't you see?"

I snapped once again, "See what?"

More firmly now, "Can't you see what God is doing? He is at work all around us. He saved my life. He's given me a new life! Can't you see all that God is doing?"

Different Worlds

How can two people live in the same world, experience the same thing, and see things so differently? Could it be that we are actually living in two different worlds? While I was living in my world, Tami was living in Jesus' kingdom—his world, her life lived his way. At the same time I was living in my own little kingdom. My kingdom involved my agenda, my world, my life lived my way. It's the way I most often see and interact with the world. I am the king, the lord, and the god of my kingdom. Yet Tami was content—no, she strove—to live with her eyes focused beyond herself, on the kingdom of God.

I realized I had been carrying a weight around for months. It was like a boulder that kept me from moving on, kept me stuck between my grief and my anger. I carried this weight past that corner every day unknowingly to me. It had gotten heavier every drive to work, every trip to the grocery store, and every jog around the block. I thought I knew how the kingdom of Jesus worked. I thought the bad people among us got what they deserved and the good people lived in the protective shelter of a loving, peaceful Jesus. As long as we obeyed the rules and followed the laws, we would be safe. Right? But with Tami's words, I realized how heavy the stone was becoming. My religion, my desire to maintain a certain moral standing and accomplish specific disciplines, my false sense of what is right had blinded me to the simplicity of Jesus. Tami's words reminded me that if I were going to live the Jesus way, I would have to put down my religious stone and look beyond it, opening my eyes to a whole new kingdom.

Opening Our Eyes

There's a lot to see when we look past our religion and focus our attention on Jesus and his ways. As we open our eyes, the kingdom of heaven comes into focus, and we are surrounded by its nearness. Jesus' invitation to participate in it becomes real. There is no limit to what God is doing in our world. With eyes wide open we realize that we are in the middle of it. How could we have missed it? It's clear that Jesus didn't come simply to tell us how to get to heaven; he came to show us that heaven might come to earth *through* us as we follow him.

The kingdom of God is within our reach. God is present, and he has invited us into his presence. God is at work, and he has invited us into his activity. God is active in loving the world, and he invites us to love and be loved.

Imagine what would happen if we began to view our lives through the lens of Jesus. Imagine if we could see the kingdom at work as clearly as Jesus saw it. Imagine a way of living in which each morning we awoke to the reality that Jesus is alive and at work all around us, inviting us into his kingdom. That's exactly what Tami was trying to get me to see when she said, "Can't you see what God is doing?" This way of living can be the difference between daylight and darkness. This is what happens when we engage with Jesus on a daily basis. He leads. We follow. He is at work and he shows us his way.

Divine Encounters

I have some good friends who are constantly having what they call divine encounters. They are the ordinary moments in each day that become much more, and they are always talking about them. I thought they had an inordinate number of these kinds of moments, especially considering that similar experiences are few and far between for me. Frankly, I was a little bit jealous, thinking that maybe God didn't love me enough to give me the same kind of experiences.

But I realized that Tami has those kinds of God-moments too. Recently we were on a road trip and stopped at a hotel for the evening. She went to the lobby for a few minutes and came back with two men she had met at the front desk, men who were on their way to Myrtle Beach for Bike Week. You'll understand if this caught me a bit off guard. According to Tami, they had blown out the radiator in the SUV pulling their motorcycle trailer. As it turned out, they live in the same community we do, were now staying in the same hotel we were (in the town where Tami and I grew up, no less), standing at the front desk at the same time Tami was, and talking about a hobby (motorcycling) we both enjoy. As she struck up a conversation, she discovered they needed a ride to an auto parts store a few miles down the road, but because the town had no cab service, they didn't know how they would get there. Ever watchful for an opportunity to live like Jesus, Tami offered our services in taking them to the store. The next morning, we delayed our trip a couple of hours while I ran them around town, picking up parts.

Jesus was inviting us to join him in loving and serving, and all I would see was my world being invaded and messed up. While I was a little flustered that my early morning plans had been altered, Tami was ecstatic to have a chance to serve these two new friends. Once again, I recognize my unlimited capacity for limited sight while Tami keeps her gaze focused on the kingdom of God. What I saw as a disruption in my schedule, she saw as a divine opportunity to serve. She quickly connects the events of the day with what God is doing and willingly jumps on board with every chance. I began to understand that the problem wasn't that God didn't offer me these divine encounters, but I just didn't see them. My stone of religion was too large to see over, so while I spent my time staring down the must-dos of professional Christianity, my wife saw the unlimited opportunity to live with Jesus.

It is so easy to get caught up in living like Jesus and turn it into a mantra. When we do this, we become like the Pharisees. Instead of allowing Jesus to live his life through us in the power of his Spirit, we start measuring ourselves based on how good we are. Living like Jesus is about allowing him to live in and through us. It is not we who live, but it is Jesus who lives through us.

It's His Kingdom

As I am rediscovering the simplicity of Jesus and his ways, my eyes are opening to these opportunities, and I am beginning to see them more and more frequently. The decision to live this way is intentional, and it's a choice I must make every day. Once again it begins with my prayer, *Show me your way.* That's exactly what Jesus was doing when in teaching his disciples to pray he said, "Lord, let your Kingdom come, your will be done on earth—in and through my life—today as it is in heaven" (Matt. 6:9–10, author paraphrase).

A good starting point in making this decision is understanding what Jesus meant by the word *kingdom*. What is his kingdom, and what does it mean to have it come to earth? *Kingdom* can be translated as the "reign of God." God's kingdom comes to earth when God reigns supreme in our lives and in our world. His kingdom comes when we hear his voice and we see him at work. His kingdom comes when we join him in what he is doing in this world. His kingdom comes when we live like Jesus, love like Jesus, and leave what Jesus left behind in the power of his Spirit.

At the same time, even living like Jesus, loving like Jesus, and leaving what Jesus left behind can become a religion when we fail to hear his voice and see him at work in this world. Living the Jesus way should always include a response to following him. He doesn't join us in our world; we join him in his world. When this happens his kingdom comes.

The kingdom Jesus spoke about is not complex or mysterious, even though it contains mystery. It is simply my life lived God's way in full surrender to him in the context of his people and his mission. When we awake each day with the determination to join Jesus in his work, we awake into his kingdom. When our mission is to discover Jesus in every interaction throughout the day, we live in his kingdom. When we realize that Jesus lived his life so we might see how to live our lives, we approach his kingdom. When we live like Jesus, love like Jesus, and leave what Jesus left behind, we are furthering his kingdom. When I recognize that each day I must decrease and allow Jesus to increase, I am helping bring his kingdom to earth.

The kingdom begins with hearing his voice as we come to understand him as the way, the truth, and the life. As we read his Word, we come to understand him and his ways. As we listen to his Spirit, we come to experience him in an intimate way. His ways becomes our ways, his truth becomes our truth, and his life becomes our life.

At the same time the kingdom is not all about me. The kingdom begins with understanding Jesus' mission, and it's all about me joining Jesus—his kingdom, his mission on earth. His mission is one of peace: peace with God and peace with people. In finding peace with God, we are forgiven, loved, and served by God in Jesus. This peace continues when we share it with people—forgiving, loving, and serving our enemies. Jesus came to reconcile the world to the Father and to show us a whole new way of living with one another. It's a way that can be characterized by peace. His Sermon on the Mount points us to his manifesto of peace. His life shows us the way of peace. His commission—our Great Commission—gives us the mission of peace.

In drawing near to Jesus we experience his life, and out of the overflow of this life we join him in his mission of peace.

When we live like Jesus, we come to understand that his kingdom is like a mustard seed. What begins as the smallest act of faith soon becomes so much more when we follow Jesus.

DAY 4: FINDING THE JESUS WAY

1. What did Jesus mean when he said, "The kingdom of heaven is near"?
2. What does joining God in his kingdom look like for you?
3. How could letting Jesus lead your life bring peace into your relationships and ultimately peace on earth?

Thoughts, Prayers, and Doodles on the Jesus Way

_____

_____

_____

_____

_____

_____

_____

_____

_____

_____

_____

_____

_____

CHAPTER 5

Journey . . . It's Hard to Travel Sitting

*"The thief comes only to steal and kill and destroy; I have
come that they may have life, and have it to the full."*
—John 10:10

> **Toxic Religion:** We reduce our relationship with
> God down to a few moments each day.
>
> **The Jesus Way:** Jesus invites us into a 24/7
> relationship.

Lately something has been unsettling me. It started recently
when I heard one of our pastors teach about having a regular
time with God. Following his teaching, I got up and asked
the question of those there, "How many of you get this?" "How
many of you are the kind of disciplined, organized, methodical
people who get up, day in and day out, and begin each and every day
with a special quiet time with God?" One person raised his hand.
Granted, this was one of our campuses and didn't represent our

entire congregation. Also, the question was sort of spontaneous, so I caught all the disciplined, organized, methodical people off guard, which may have temporarily overloaded their system causing them to freeze in the moment. Following my first question I went on to ask, "How many of you are like me—your ADD has ADHD?" Overwhelmingly the majority raised their hands. It was apparent that most of us really struggled with the mastery of this morning discipline we religious types have come to refer to as a quiet time.

Before we go any further, I'm not mad or angry at people who are overly structured, and represent the 2 percent of people who are disciplined, organized, and methodical and actually do quiet time 7 days a week, 365 weeks a year, every year of their lives. I think it's a great idea and can be an important discipline in our lives.

However, I am concerned and even angry (the kind of anger Jesus had when he tossed the religious crowd out of the temple) over the religious yoke we put on people by reducing our relationship with him to a brief time each morning, called a quiet time, where we sit, read, write, and ponder the mysteries of God. Is this whole idea of a quiet time a really good thing, or is it one of those yokes I talked about earlier that proves to be a heavy burden keeping us from experiencing the presence and joy of following Jesus?

Here's my confession: I don't have a quiet time every morning, nor do I ever want to get to the point that I reduce my relationship with Jesus to a few minutes of alone time with him each day. Matter of fact, I didn't have a quiet time today. I woke up, held my wife really close (I'm going on an overnighter), got up, and jumped into my writing. Long before I got up, I sensed Jesus leading me to get right to my writing, capturing what he had been saying to me. That's what I'm doing. I don't feel guilty about it either. Matter of fact, I feel free and really close to Jesus this morning. I feel that he is speaking, and in the midst of our fellowship I am trying to capture my experience so you can benefit from it as well.

Regular Time with God Is Important

Before I go any further let me say that I do try to spend regular time with God most mornings. I really do think it can and should be an important part of one's relationship with him. When I fail to have a regular time with God, I tend to drift, and my drifting results in losing my way. At the same time, I never want my routine to become so mundane that it simply becomes something I do. That's what I mean by religion. If I'm completely honest, there are times I go a few weeks when the morning thing is easy. Then there are seasons when I am sporadic at best. Finally, there are other times, like this morning, when God has been so clear and loud in my life that to pause for a few moments of quiet time wouldn't be right. God has already spoken and I simply need to follow.

I really believe all this is part of having a relationship with Jesus. There is far more to my relationship with Jesus than a brief time each morning with him when I read Scriptures, confess sins, and say prayers. Our relationship with Jesus is our life. Just as life is real, my relationship with him is real. It's a little like the stock market with all of its ebb and flow. Some days it is up and other days it is down, but if you look at the trend over a long period of time, and since its inception hopefully, it is up. However, when we realize that we are living this kind of up-and-down—two steps forward, one back—life in the context of grace, there is an incredible amount of freedom with it. Do you realize that there is nothing in heaven or on earth that can separate us from the love of God, and now that we are in Christ, there isn't now, nor will there ever be any condemnation? That's pretty amazing. Excuse me while I dance!

I would be the first to admit that we are prone to drift and lose our way. After all, at the core of the matter we all have the sin problem, and sin, according to the apostle Paul, is our propensity to miss the mark. I am constantly losing my way when it comes to this journey called life. I am forgiven. I am free. I can never be condemned again. At the same time, I drift. Which is why having a regular time early in the morning to re-center our relationship with Jesus makes perfectly good sense.

When I understand this, my motivation for having a regular time changes. I understand my need to stay close to him. I understand I tend to drift. I understand like any relationship in our noisy world I have to fight for intimacy. I have a new motivation. It's not that I have checked off a list of spiritual exercises or expectations in order to be right with God. I can't live a moment detached from the Vine. I need intimacy with him. I was created for it. I want to stay really close, so I check in.

Life Is a Journey

The metaphor we often use to describe our relationship with Jesus is the word *journey*. If we are to follow him this word makes sense. We are on a journey, but the journey we are on is not my journey, it is his journey. This a good thing since we are so challenged in our relationships these days. If it is his journey, then he leads and I follow.

Speaking of journey, Tami and I enjoy riding motorcycles. It's something we do most weekends when the weather and time allow it. The other day I was surfing—not the kind that requires going outside and getting on a board, but the kind I can do from my easy chair with a remote. She spoke up and asked me if I wanted to go riding. That's all it took. We were off and cruising. The interesting thing about riding a motorcycle in the north Georgia mountains is you really do just ride. You don't necessarily have a destiny; you simply live in the moment, taking it all in. Sometimes that can present a challenge. After all I'm a man so I need a destiny, a hill to climb, a target to hit, or something that releases an emotional cocktail in my nervous systems and gives me a kind of rush or sense of accomplishment.

I asked her whether she wanted to go north or south as we took off. She didn't have a preference so I went north. We came to a cross-roads where we usually go west, but I decided to venture outside my comfort zone and went east. About an hour later we ended up at a resort mountain town filled with life. Entire parking lots were filled with motorcycles; you would have thought it was Bikers' Week. We parked, surveyed the area, and ended up at a watering hole by a mountain stream that consisted of an outdoor pavilion with a grill, bar, dance floor, live band, and about two hundred of our closest biker friends. I say closest biker friends, because bikers share a common bond that makes us all brothers.

We hung out, caught up on life, watched families float together down the mountain stream, ate our food, admired the bikes, listened to the music, and then made our way back down the mountain. We had a blast. We did life. It was a good journey.

There is power in the word *journey* when we use it to describe our relationship with Jesus. That's why part of my rethinking has involved going back and rereading the Gospels over and over again. I mentioned earlier that we invite Jesus into our lives, that's a good thing, but at some point we need to stop inviting and start following. He has invited us to follow him. Following him means he is the leader and I am a follower. He is the Vine, I am a branch. My life, my strength, my direction, and my purpose all come from being intimately attached to him. As he goes I must go. I go by following his voice. He is my shepherd and as his sheep I hear his voice and I respond. When I re-center my life on a regular basis, through a regular time with him, I hear him and I follow. That's my motivation for a quiet time. It's not a religious activity I do in order to check it off a list. It is the result of this incredible journey of following him. I don't want to miss what he is doing in, around, or through me.

It's not enough to simply have a quiet time, but I must learn to abide in him. Abiding in him means following him all day, every day. This requires regularly checking in with him because of my tendency to wander and lose my way. When I follow him, he leads me to many watering holes of life. The journey is filled with many stopping-over places where life happens.

A Brief Watering Hole Called Grace

That's what happened to me today. A friend from Europe called. We have a track record. We have been friends and partners in mission for a long time. We chatted about the future . . . what God is doing in his life and in mine. As we were winding down our conversation, I thanked him for what he was doing. My daughter was in Madrid because of him. I pointed this out to him. I sensed Jesus telling me to encourage him. I told him that she wouldn't be there if he hadn't first gone. She wouldn't. In the middle of our conversation I received a text from her. It read "Hey, Dad! How are you? Things are good here! Just eating lunch! I get to meet my intercambio (online relationship with a Spaniard from Madrid) tomorrow! Just wanted to say hey and I love you!" I read it to Larry. We said good-bye. Don't miss the connection. This was a divine appointment. Following Jesus this morning allowed me to be part of God encouraging my friend. My daughter was part of it and didn't even know it. This was my watering hole as I followed him.

When we abide in him, our day is filled with similar encounters. We never know what we might encounter. The kingdom of heaven is really near. Yes, it's true that sometimes I see but don't see, and others times I hear but don't hear or understand. Today I made the connection because I was following.

How do we follow? How do we stay connected? How do we hear from the Father? It begins when we touch base in the mornings, but it doesn't end there. What do we do with the other twenty-three hours and forty-five minutes each day? How do we check in? How do we follow the apostle Paul's example and pray without ceasing? Asking these questions helps us realize that following Jesus on this journey called life involves more than a simple stopping-over point each morning. "Remain in me, I will remain in you" (John 15:4 NIV). It involves a lifetime of intimacy that begins fresh each morning. I've got to go. I've got a journey to take today, and I can't wait to see where it leads.

DAY 5: FINDING THE JESUS WAY

1. Take a moment and reflect on the last time you clearly heard Jesus speaking to you. What did you hear him saying? How did you respond?

2. What are the advantages and disadvantages of a regular time alone with God?

3. How can your time alone with God set you up for following him all day long?

4. What does "abiding" in Jesus look like for you?

Thoughts, Prayers, and Doodles on the Jesus Way

CHAPTER 6

Frozen . . . Just Hit the Send Button!

*And teaching them to obey everything I have commanded you.
And surely I am with you always, to the very end of the age.*
—Matthew 28:20

Toxic Religion: God is way out there and hard to touch.

The Jesus Way: Jesus is really close and wants to have a relationship with us.

I sat there frozen in time. All I had to do was type two words and press send and a writing project I had been working on for months would be completed. I couldn't do it. Time stood still. Questions swirled around my overactive mind. I was writing the dedication in my last book. I had decided to dedicate it to my son. He was in Afghanistan. He was due to be home in a few months. I had already typed the words with pride, "This book is dedicated to my son who has spent the last fifteen months in Afghanistan serving with the 82nd Airborne." All I lacked were two words, but I was frozen by fear and anxiety. The words I struggled to type were "Welcome home!" That's it. That's all I had left to finish the book.

I paused. I was pondering a heavy and painful question, *What if he doesn't come home?* I had gotten those dreaded phone calls three times since his deployment. They all had to do with terrible explosions: an IED, a rocket, and an ambush. Things were heating up. The few times I got to speak to my son on the phone, I could hear the concern in his own voice. Here I was face-to-face with my fear and it was immobilizing me. We were squared off. I felt fear's ugly, cold grip around my heart. I was in pain. I wanted to write those words. I needed to write those words. That's when I heard a voice. It was a peaceful voice: *He will be home. Trust me. If he doesn't come back to you, he will be with me in heaven. Either way he will be home. Type those words.* With tears streaming down my face I typed those final two words W-e-l-c-o-m-e H-o-m-e! The Father had spoken. I sensed his peace and his presence. I had my answer. I pressed the "send" button on my computer. By some mysterious way my manuscript made its way digitally to my publisher.

That's just the beginning of the story. Finally, after months, we received the phone call we had dreamed of. Our son had been extracted by helicopter from the battle zone. He was safe at an undisclosed place in the Middle East. We weren't sure when he would be on his way, but he was safe. A brief stay at this location and a little detoxing of his own, and he would be headed home.

It took weeks, but finally the day arrived when his plane landed at Fort Pope, North Carolina. Three hundred soldiers returned from the 82nd Airborne, 4-73 Cavalry Reconnaissance Unit. We gathered, along with hundreds of other family members, to welcome our soldiers home. There with us were the wounded soldiers who had been sent home earlier, newborn babies who had never been held by their soldier dads, mothers, fathers, brothers, sisters, aunts, uncles, neighbors, friends, sweethearts, politicians, commanding officers, reporters, and veterans in a massive welcome home party. It was like a scene out of the movies, only better.

There we all stood, intoxicated by the moment, with banners, flags, posters, media, cameras, videos, bands—all part of that incredible moment. After fifteen hard months the brave soldiers of the 82nd Airborne were lining up in formation to make the march up the tarmac to their family and friends. The band began to play. I thought I saw my son. I did; he was third from the left about three-quarters through the formation. His stern military expression broke with a smile as he saw me in the crowd. I was the one jumping up and down, screaming like a wild man. No one noticed.

A rope separated us from our soldiers. The band struck a chord and played "The Star Spangled Banner." Finally the commanding officer barked out a few final orders and announced the mission of the 82nd Airborne, 4-73 Cavalry Reconnaissance Unit accomplished. The heroes of the 82nd had completed their mission. For the first time in fifteen months they were dismissed. We went wild. My son, our sons, had returned home.

Later that day we began to make the trip back to Atlanta with our son in tow to our home where he had learned to drive, where he had run track, camped out in the backyard, played hours of video games, and sat in his room drawing the most amazing and intricate pictures. It was there that he had taught himself to play the guitar and spent hours entertaining us with the songs he wrote about life.

When we arrived, several boxes awaited me in our foyer. They were from my publisher. The first copies of my book had been released and a neighbor put them just inside the door. I immediately opened one of the boxes and took the book out and there it was, "This book is dedicated to my son who spent the last fifteen months in Afghanistan serving with the 82nd Airborne. **Welcome home!**" I read it to him. My son had returned home (excuse me while I get the tears out of my eyes).

Don't Miss It!

Could God have been any louder? When I opened that door and found my book, it was as if God was standing there in front of me and my son, saying, "Welcome home!" I don't think he could have been louder! Not even if he had been standing in the door handing me the book.

What if God is really closer than we think? I mean what if he has been here all the time or he is here all the time, but we keep missing him? What if this thing called religion keeps getting in the way of the life God has for each of us? What if we could do a little repenting, followed by a little rethinking, resulting in a little reliving, that included a God who is not way out there, but really near? What if we discovered that all along the problem isn't a God who can't be touched, but the problem is our understanding of that God?

That's exactly what we see in the Gospels. On one occasion Philip, one of the closest followers, raises this very issue when he makes this statement to Jesus, "Lord, show us the Father and that will be enough for us" (John 14:8). What appears to be an innocent question at first gets an unexpected response from Jesus. "Don't you know me, Philip, even after I have been among you such a long time? Anyone who has seen me has seen the Father. How can you say, 'Show us the father'?" (14:9).

The Father had been with Philip all along. Jesus couldn't believe what he was hearing. How did Philip miss him? How do we miss him?

Let's go back to the earlier chapters. Jesus invites us to *come, follow him*. He begins his ministry by inviting us to *repent, for the kingdom of heaven is near*. Recently after speaking on the kingdom of heaven, someone told me he didn't realize the kingdom of heaven was near. He thought it was way out there—something that is going to happen in the future (he had been reading too many end-time novels). Yet Jesus tells us it is near. He taught that even though seeing and hearing, we wouldn't hear or understand his kingdom. We can't separate Jesus and his kingdom. Where Jesus reigns, his kingdom comes. It can and should come in our lives every moment of every day. Learning to follow him assures our living out his kingdom in and through our lives. When we remain in him and he in us, his kingdom comes. Living in his kingdom is a surefire way to detox from religion.

Jesus Is Right Here, Not Way Out There

When my son was in Afghanistan, I thought of him almost every moment of every day. I made decisions I knew would impact him and our family in a positive way. I made plans that would impact us and prepare us for his return. The same is true when I allow God's kingdom to invade my life every day. I learn to hear his voice and see his activity. When I hear and see him, I understand this is his invitation to follow.

Unlike my son, Jesus never leaves us alone. He is always with us. He is with us in that he leaves us his Spirit.

> If you love me, you will obey what I command. And I will
> ask the Father, and he will give you another Counselor
> to be with you forever—the Spirit of truth, . . . for he
> lives with you and will be in you. I will not leave you as
> orphans; I will come to you. Before long, the world will
> not see me anymore, but you will see me. Because I live,
> you also will live. On that day you will realize that I am in
> my Father, and you are in me, and I am in you. Whoever
> has my commands and obeys them, he is the one who
> loves me. He who loves me will be loved by my Father, and
> I too will love him and show myself to him.
> (John 14:15–21)

Because he lives in us now and we are one, we come to hear and see him in a number of ways.

We experience him in the ordinary things and moments of each day.

We see him in the spit and mud when he healed a blind man. We see him in the fish and loaves when he fed the five thousand. We see him in a basin of water and a towel when he washed the feet of his disciples. Jesus took ordinary stuff and did extraordinary things through them and he still does. We see him in a gentle breeze on a fall day. We hear him in the roar of the surf on a moonlit beach. We experience him in the embrace of a friend after a meaningful conversation. He was really loud one day when Tami and I paused for a quick prayer as she was dropping me off at the office. As I took her hand and bowed my head, I was so overwhelmed by his presence all I could do was sit there in silence. It was as if he were sitting right there with us. He really was.

We experience him in the moment we choose to let go of a painful past.

We experience him in the moment when we abandon the fear and anxiety of an uncertain future. In all of these ordinary moments we are reminded he is with us always, even until the end of the age.

We experience him in a passage of Scripture.

Even though we have read it time and time again, for some reason, in this moment his Word takes on new life and meaning. It carries with it healing and life. This is why it is so important that we not only pray, but we spend time reading his Word and coming to know it intimately.

Because my son is in the Army and sometimes deployed to dangerous places, I often get the question, "How do you do it?" I don't know, but I do. God speaks to me through his Word. His Word becomes his promise to me. His promise gives me hope. This hope gives me life. In my son's last deployment God spoke these words to me. "He who dwells in the shelter of the Most High will rest in the shadow of the Almighty. I will say of the LORD, 'He is my refuge and my fortress, my God, in whom I trust'" (Ps. 91:1–2). God used my cousin to speak these words into my life. She later had them engraved on a dog tag my son wore on the second half of his deployment. God spoke to me. He still does.

We experience him in ordinary opportunities to serve.

That's right, we see him in unplanned opportunities to be Jesus to someone else. I pulled in my driveway one evening and for some reason I felt like cutting the grass. Maybe it was because the rain had finally refrained, or maybe it was because of the new Cub Cadet tractor sitting in my garage. About halfway through my yard I noticed my neighbor was cutting her grass. I had been watching her grass. It was tall, thick, and unsightly. I had wanted to cut it. Not only did I want to cut it, I wanted to serve her. She had a push mower, and the work was obviously getting the best of her. I broke off my route and pulled up to her. In her broken English she tried to tell me something. When I finished cutting, she was standing there with a can of gas. I put a little in my tractor and went on to finish my grass. In that moment I felt the presence of God. His kingdom came.

I also learned that when you have the right equipment, you can serve others. I had never had the right equipment before, but when we remain in him, we have the right equipment. Because he is with us through his Spirit, we can bear fruit, and he gives us gifts to serve others. He enables and empowers us. He calls us to be his body. We are without excuse.

We experience him in time of temptation and trial.

There are opportunities all during the day to draw near to God as we face temptations and trials. "Submit yourselves, then, to God. Resist the devil, and he will flee from you" (James 4:7). Go ahead and identify your greatest temptation or trial and use it as your opportunity to check in with God. These temptations are a constant reminder of our need for God. With this fresh awareness, next time you sense an onslaught by the tempter, go ahead and submit yourself to God and resist the devil and he will flee from you. Enjoy the intimacy of victory.

We experience him in times of peace in spite of chaos and adversity.

Whenever I am facing challenging and difficult times, I know I am going to experience him. That's what I experienced in the opening story about my son in this chapter. "Welcome home!" I experienced God's presence.

Recently I received a phone call from my sister. She was upset. It was Mom. She was in the hospital, recovering from a knee replacement procedure. Something had happened. Her breathing was labored, she couldn't wake up, and her thoughts were incoherent. The doctors thought the worst. "We think she might have had a stroke. You need to come." That's when I heard the Father speak. What I heard him saying was that my mom would have it no other way. She was a fighter, having spent years expecting a cure to a malignant blood disorder as a patient at the famous M. D. Anderson Research Hospital. The doctors gave her five years to live twenty-five years ago. Now they have all but announced a cure for the very disease she has been fighting. It hasn't been easy, but as I said, she is a fighter.

I understood what I sensed God was saying to me. Even if it were the worst, Mom would have it no other way. In spite of the risk, she would have still had the surgery. This is one woman who is not going to spend the rest of her life confined to closed spaces because she can't get around. I felt God's peace. I knew he was present. He always is.

Mom is rebounding! That's one tough woman who knows how to live life.

Living life begins each day and ends each day with Jesus. Jesus desires to be in every moment and every part of our day. This is the Jesus way.

DAY 6: FINDING THE JESUS WAY

1. When was the last time God spoke to you through an ordinary circumstance?
2. What Scripture passage or verse of Scripture has God used to speak to you?
3. When was the last time you had a divine encounter or opportunity to be a "little Jesus" to someone?
4. Pause right now. Listen! What do you hear? What is Jesus telling you? What does following him mean to you today?

Thoughts, Prayers, and Doodles on the Jesus Way

_____

_____

_____

_____

_____

_____

_____

_____

_____

_____

_____

_____

_____

_____

_____

_____

_____

_____

_____

_____

_____

_____

CHAPTER 7

Blessed . . . Living a Different Kind of Dream

*"Blessed are the poor in spirit, for theirs is
the kingdom of heaven."*

—Matthew 5:3

> **Toxic Religion:** My success is an indication of God's favor.
>
> **The Jesus Way:** Jesus is our life, and nothing else can satisfy.

'm living the dream." It's a common response among my Western Christian friends when I ask how they're doing. Without an exception I have this kind of reaction in my spirit when I hear this. Rather than launching into an inquisition about whose dream, exactly, they're living, I assume they are talking about the idyllic American dream. I assume they mean they have a good job, make good money, live in a luxurious home (compared to the rest of the world's standards), have two or three kids playing soccer, vote their convictions during most elections, give their surplus to Goodwill, take a couple of well-planned vacations each year, are enjoying good health, say the Pledge of Allegiance on occasion, enjoy religious freedom, spend currency that reads "In God we trust," and attend weekly religious services (they may even attend a really cool church).

It's not that this is wrong, but we can have all this and still nudge Jesus out of our lives. The challenge is God has a dream for our lives that doesn't depend on any of this. The dream I just described is often short-lived. As a matter of fact, even as I write, this country— the America of American dream—is facing an economic meltdown, we are locked in two wars, we are experiencing an all-time low point in our global political relationships, and our children no longer have a Christian worldview. Meanwhile, God has a higher and better dream for our lives that he has revealed through Jesus, a dream that fulfills our true purpose and destiny. Apart from Jesus, there is no dream, but when we live, love, and leave what he left behind, there is no escaping it.

Heaven in a Strange Place

On a recent trip to Africa, our team leader had an incredible idea. We hosted a goat roast in honor of our new Malawian friends. It felt like a scene right out of the Gospels as the goats were slaughtered, roasted, and served with rice, beans, and sema (a kind of corn similar to grits). After days of bartering, gathering, slaughtering, and preparing, the food was ready. It was a feast fit for a king (or at least a village chief), and guests came from everywhere. There was electricity and excitement in the late afternoon African air—this kind of celebration was a first for us, as well as for the people of the village. They felt honored to attend and we were honored to host. We ate until we were full, speaking with one another about the kinship that superseded continents, dialects, and skin color. When our celebration came to an end, we followed our local guides and headed back to our rooms on foot. It was only a few hundred yards away, but it was dark in the Valley of the Snakes, and precaution was in order. Cobras, vipers, black mambas, and pythons roam freely.

Our guides that night were six young Malawian children, somewhere between the ages of five and eight years old. They knew the way and traveled the rocky terrain with ease. As the children lead us through the valley, they sang at the tops of their voices, some of the most harmonic sounds I have ever heard. I couldn't understand their native tongue, but the words were secondary to the emotion that accompanied them. It was along that rocky path in the middle of the Valley of the Snakes that I witnessed what I think it really means to be blessed. What I experienced that night was nothing short of pure joy. I had never experienced that kind of joy before, unbridled and passionate in the midst of difficult circumstances. I was overwhelmed, and their joy soon became my joy.

Here I was in one of the poorest places in the world. The kids were barefoot. Many of them had lost their parents to AIDS. Their water supply was limited, and what little they had was dirty and diseased. The clothes they wore looked like hand-me-downs that the Salvation Army would have thrown away. Their skin was covered with the dust and grime of many days. Their opportunity for a secondary education was severely limited, and whether they would even have a next meal was in doubt. Yet in that moment I experienced heaven on earth. I really did! The kingdom came to earth as it was in heaven. There was no pride or ego, no embarrassment, no shame—sin vanished and heaven came. It was absolutely amazing in the most literal sense of the term, and I now know a little bit about what heaven will be like because I caught a glimpse of it that night.

I was stunned, but not just by the children's exuberant joy. I was stunned that I have never known that kind of joy myself. Sure, I've been happy before. I'd even go so far as to say I've been joyful. But my life has been comfortable, well fed, disease-free, warm, protected from rain and snow, and surrounded by friends and family. Who wouldn't be joyful in that kind of situation? Yet these children sang as they walked through the Valley of the Snakes—a fitting description of their entire lives. Perhaps they're living a different kind of dream.

Jesus' Way Revealed

Living the Jesus way requires a new dream that can be achieved only through a redemptive imagination. Stop and pause for a moment. Reflect on the world and your place in it. Answer this question, "If the kingdom of God was to come right here, right now, and God had his way in this place, circumstance, or situation, what would it be like?" Maybe you are reflecting on your own challenges. Better yet, maybe your mind has shifted to an issue in your community or beyond to the world. Recently I began to dream about a hundred drinking wells and irrigation systems in Africa. Maybe you are dreaming about peace within your family, community, or world. God gives us this gift of imagination to use for his good. He gives it to us to tap into his goodness and desire for the redemption of every element of his creation.

We have this redemptive imagination when we see the world through Jesus' eyes. The gateway to this kind of redemptive imagination is found in the Sermon on the Mount (see Matt. 5–7). I think I could spend the rest of my life studying this passage and would only begin to understand some of its implications. Here Jesus explains what it really means to be blessed—and it is radically, dramatically different from what these followers thought they knew. Over and over again in this teaching, Jesus calls "blessed" those who dare to go against their traditional religion and live the Jesus way. Jesus turns everything upside down!

Blessed

What is blessedness? Jesus' contemporaries had long heard the religious scholars and priests enumerate the hundreds of laws they were required to keep in order to achieve a blessed status. Likewise, there seems to be a fair amount of confusion about what it means to live blessed in America. Is it good health? Is it about prosperity? You'll be hard-pressed to find a health-and-wealth theology in Jesus' words unless you consider a cross healthy and no place to lay your head wealthy. Yet, as Jesus introduced the Beatitudes, he pronounced those "blessed" who are poor in spirit, who mourn, who are persecuted, who are meek, and who are peacemakers (Matt. 5:3–10). These probably aren't considered the luckiest people in town in any generation, let alone one in which Caesar rules and Herod dominates. Jesus' teaching required that his followers abandon their previously held notions of blessedness and adopt his way of truth. In this context, blessed is the result of God's presence and approval of their lives. To be blessed is to be in a relationship with Jesus. We are truly blessed when we walk with him in this life. Through this teaching, we discover that Jesus' sense of blessing is not at all based on living *our* dream, but is an internal state of contentment that is possible for all who live *his* dream. Jesus, like the children of the Malawian village, knows that God is much more concerned with the state of our hearts and minds than our standard of living.

I learned this lesson early in my ministry as I experienced a difficult time in leading a congregation. We were in the Deep South at a time when prejudice was a standard Christian virtue (I think it still is in some places). Things seemed to be going well until I began bringing some African-American children into the church from other parts of our community. All of a sudden, my leadership wasn't as stable as it had been, and I began to experience a great deal of disapproval. Things heated up, and some people really got ugly about things. It seemed there was a good bit of unwritten "law" pervading our church culture, and I was breaking it.

One night during this time, I received a phone call from my sister. She was concerned about what we were going through and wanted me to know that she was praying for Tami and me. I quoted part of the Beatitudes: "Blessed are you when people insult you, persecute you and falsely say all kinds of evil against you because of me. Rejoice and be glad, because great is your reward in heaven, for in the same way they persecuted the prophets who were before you" (Matt. 5:11–12). I told her I considered it a real honor and blessing to suffer for Jesus. I meant it. She went on to say, "David, this may sound weird, but I envy you."

I can't explain it, but I know I was experiencing the kind of thing Jesus spoke of, and as time passed I began to understand even more that living like Jesus, even when all the props of religion are knocked out from under you, is a blessed experience.

Sometimes we must confront the brutal facts. Jesus' kingdom and his dream for our lives are radically different from what we have heard or thought. Later in the Sermon on the Mount, Jesus repeats several times, "You have heard it said . . . But I tell you . . ." Living like Jesus means unlearning our old religious ways and relearning his ways, and not only rethinking but redreaming. In his teaching you will find no recipe for a safe life. In contrast, he invites us to come and die—not once, but daily. He doesn't take us out of this mess of life, but he invites us to follow and walk with him in this life. He promises us that our right-side-up world will be turned upside down, and our outside-in approach to life will be turned inside out. No wonder he began his ministry with a simple message of repentance; there was a lot of wrong to be undone.

Jesus' followers knew the Torah (the first five books of Moses); they had read about God's blessing on Adam and Eve to be fruitful and fill the earth (Gen. 1:22). They knew of his promise to Abraham to bless all nations through him (Gen. 12:3). They knew his blessing was extended to the Israelites that they were to be a light to the nations (Isa. 49:6). Over time, however, the word *blessed* came to be associated with right and better living. If you live right, you are blessed. Blessed people have more and better things than others. It's a lot like living the dream. You have it better and more abundantly than your neighbor, and living blessed is an external condition, the result of right living and right status. Yet Jesus came teaching quite the opposite. When he talked about blessing, he was speaking of an inward contentment in spite of external circumstances. It didn't matter if you had enough to eat, if you were warm at night, or if your family died. Being blessed means knowing and following Jesus and being a light of love and hope in this world.

This explains the pure joy I experienced in Africa with the children. "Blessed are the poor in spirit"—these children seemingly had nothing to be excited about. "Blessed are those who mourn"—many of these children had mourned their parents and siblings and other relatives. "Blessed are the meek"—who wouldn't consider these children humble. What's more, they experienced the joys and blessings that Jesus promised all who live his way. Theirs is the kingdom of heaven, right here on earth. They are comforted by the power of the Holy Spirit and the love of their community. And though they are poor in spirit, they are rich as they obtain the fullness of life in Christ.

In order to have Jesus' life, we have to give up our lives. This is the Jesus way—it may seem like a paradox, but we must understand that God's economy is vastly different from our own. I know a lot of people who have lived the dream. They made it, they were successful, they were in control. Yet they have cashed in the dream and walked away from it in favor of something far better. They have traded their dream for Jesus' dream, and they are coming alive with new life as a result.

God's dream for our lives begins on the inside as it is planted, watered, and grows like a mustard seed into something much bigger than anyone thought. There is no stopping it, as everything takes on new meaning and fresh purpose. God's kingdom comes into focus as our lives blossom and motivations yield to inspirations. God's kingdom comes when we seek first his ways. When we live, love, and leave like Jesus, we are blessed.

We Are the Ones in Need

I saw a beautiful glimpse of God's dream for us that night in the children. When I tell people about these kids, I am often asked, "What do they need?" "Is there anything we can do for them?" "What do we have that can make their lives better?" They don't need anything from us. *We* are the ones in need. If we gave them what we have, they would become like us. *We* need what *they* have. We need unfettered joy in the midst of tragedy. We need grace and peace when that's all we have to live on. We need simplicity and a heart that rejoices in Christ alone. Yes, they need clean water, food, and good medical care. But they don't need us to begin propping their lives up with all the stuff and complexity we think our lives require. These things that we think give life are merely stumbling blocks to the real life Jesus offers.

Repeatedly Jesus invites us to learn from these and other children: "I tell you the truth, unless you change and become like little children, you will never enter the kingdom of heaven. Therefore, whoever humbles himself like this child is the greatest in the kingdom of heaven" (Matt. 18:3–4).

It's not the powerful who are blessed. It's not the strong. It's not those who have it all together. It's not those who have all the stuff. It's the opposite. It's not what you think.

DAY 7: FINDING THE JESUS WAY

1. Whose dream are you living?
2. What does God's blessing look like in your life?
3. What can we learn from these children?

Thoughts, Prayers, and Doodles on the Jesus Way

CHAPTER 8

Margin . . . Making Room for What Matters

"Let us go somewhere else—to the nearby villages—so I can preach there also. That is why I have come."
—Mark 1:38

Toxic Religion: The more I do for God, the more I love God and the more he loves me.

The Jesus Way: Following Jesus involves simplifying my life in order that I make room for Jesus: his life, his love, and his mission.

E verything seems backward in the medical world. The test results were negative. But negative is positive and positive is negative, so when the test results are negative, it's a positive thing. I was lying in a hospital bed when this was explained to me, having undergone a battery of tests in the previous twenty-four hours and becoming a human pin cushion in the process. Come to think of it, everything is backward in the spiritual world.

It started months earlier when life came rushing at me like a runaway freight train. First there was a satellite call from Afghanistan; it was from my son who had been hit by an IED. His injuries were superficial, at least the ones we could account for. Later I received a second phone call, this one was from my daughter. Her college boyfriend had died during surgery to remove a cancerous tumor. I'd never seen two people enjoy each other as much as they did, but now at the age of twenty he was dead and my daughter was standing toe-to-toe with the ugly villain of grief.

At the same time, a lot of good stuff was happening in our church and ministry. The church was running at a breakneck speed with our first multisite campus, our attendance was pushing two thousand, and our World Care ministry was growing exponentially. Our partnerships in the Middle East, Africa, the Caribbean, and elsewhere around the world were blossoming with possibilities. Meanwhile, the church-planting ministry I cofounded with my good friend and partner in ministry was gaining momentum and requiring more and more of my time. Life was flying past me, and I was thriving on the activity.

A Religious Crash

At least, I thought I was. Between the tragedies beyond my control and the busyness within my control, I had taken little time to process, to rest, to refresh. Sound familiar? I'll bet it does. Most of us are hurrying through life at an alarming speed. We rush and we're not even sure why. We hurry and fret and accelerate toward an unidentifiable end, with little or no time to recover in between hits of adrenaline.

For months I had been fighting fatigue. Two years earlier my doctor had recommended I begin taking blood pressure medication. I negotiated a deal with him, committing to control my blood pressure myself and bring it down through lifestyle modification, rest, and diet. That worked for about six months. Over time I backslid from a disciplined lifestyle, and my blood pressure crept higher than ever. This time there was no negotiation. The doctor walked in with my new medication and muttered something like, "Take it in the morning and evening and have a nice day."

Now, just a few weeks later, I thought I was dying. I had a sharp pain in my chest. I felt faint, the kind of faint when your whole body starts to shut down. I couldn't think straight. It hit when I was leading a meeting. I somehow pushed through that meeting and made it home. Frankly, it wasn't the first time I had felt this pain, but this time I couldn't ignore it as I had before. As my wife drove me to the hospital, I felt helpless. In the emergency room, it took the medical team more than three hours to bring my blood pressure down, so there wasn't any doubt I would be spending the night in a paper-thin gown in a hospital bed.

We Are All Normal

Yet twenty-four hours later, the doctors told me I was OK. My heart was normal. The thing is, busyness doesn't always show up on an electrocardiogram, even though it smacked me around and left an ugly imprint. Anxiety isn't a value they can read on a lipid panel, but it hides in my closet and jumps out at me when I least expect it. Yet I'm normal. And so are you. We don't have bionic bodies that can race and work and fight and act without consequence. We aren't superhuman androids; we are human beings, subject to the laws of physics. In my short hospital stay, I realized I had been a maniac for about six months. I was running full throttle, and it had been months since I shut down to rest. I was burning the candle at both ends up until midnight, and back again at four or five in the morning. Finally, my body had had enough.

All the while, I had been listening to an old voice in my head. It said, "I've got to do these things. It's my responsibility. If I don't, who will? If I'm going to be approved and accepted by God, I have to do this." This old voice left very little room for margin, and a life without margin will almost always lead to the emergency room. Or worse.

He's God and I'm Not

While I might be a frail human being, at least I could still hear. God became rather loud in my life as a result of my experience in the hospital, and as I reread the Gospels, I noticed the disparity between Jesus' way of living and my own. It was as if God was saying to me, "David, I designed your life to have margins." My daughter had been telling me to slow down for months, but the reality of my blood pressure drove the issue home. I could hear the words Henry Blackaby had once spoken: "He is God, and you are not." The words and ways of Jesus were like a bullhorn calling me to slow down.

Jesus accomplished so much in his short life that it might surprise you to realize he lived a life with effective margins, actually accomplishing more by doing less. For many years I have been captivated by a passage of Scripture found in the early part of Mark's gospel. Jesus had just begun his public ministry and was already approaching superstar status. The whole town had gathered at his door, each person with his own expectation of what Jesus would do for him.

Yet Mark tells us, "Very early in the morning, while it was still dark, Jesus got up, left the house and went off to a solitary place, where he prayed. Simon and his companions went to look for him, and when they found him, they exclaimed: 'Everyone is looking for you!' Jesus replied, 'Let us go somewhere else—to the nearby villages—so I can preach there also. That is why I have come'" (Mark 1:35–37).

Moving On

Do you feel the pull? "Everyone is looking for you!" I certainly can. It's a pull I have become way too familiar with. The amazing thing about this story, however, is not the pull. We expect that—Jesus was a celebrity. What is so amazing to me is Jesus' response: "Let's move on." It was as if he didn't even hear Simon's call to respond to "everyone" who was looking for him. Had Jesus healed everyone? No. Had he met every need? No. Had he fulfilled every expectation? No. But he moved on. At the end of the day, Jesus had to make a choice. Being fully man, he understood he had limits and chose to live within those limits. He was able to live life in a way that shows us the best way to live—with margin.

I love my life. I love being a follower of Jesus. I love the things I get to do. I travel around the world, developing relationships and partnerships with others who are in need. I'm on a mission to help the North American church rediscover the simplicity of Jesus. There is nothing in my life I want to give up. I love it all, but I believe there are some really good things I have to give up if I am going to live like Jesus.

I'm sure that Jesus wanted to take care of every need, but he made a decision to move on when the time was right. He didn't listen to Simon Peter tell him there was still work to be done. Jesus knew his worth, and he knew it didn't come from *doing*. He also knew the people whom he was teaching, that their lives had been lived with one rabbi after another, Pharisee after Pharisee, and countless religious scholars telling them what they had to do to be right with God. I think one of the reasons we get so caught up in *doing* is the amount of religion we have imposed on ourselves. For many of us, religion is about what can be done to meet God's approval and the approval of other people. It's about living up. We get so caught up in doing the right thing that we fail to hear and see Jesus' example. We are conditioned by time and circumstance to have to earn our way, never feeling we do enough or are good enough. We find ourselves on the treadmill of life, running faster and faster to keep up with the expectations of others. Like Simon Peter, we are overwhelmed by the pressure and expectations of the crowds. After all, "Everyone is looking for me."

It's not enough to simply follow Jesus' example. If we do, we miss the point. Jesus is offering me a chance to enter into his life, love, and rest. A powerful life is not the result of simply following his example, but it is the result of spending time with him. When we enter into a relationship with him, looking for his leadership, we experience his power, presence, and purpose. This frees us from the expectations and temptations of a busy life.

Imagine reading a book with no margins. There would be no double-spacing, no edges, and no white space between columns or even around the borders of the page. You would open a book and see nothing but an endless sea of words.

It is margin that allows us to focus on each word and enjoy the thousands of words that are knitted together into a beautiful story. The same is true of life. Margin allows us to concentrate, to focus on one thing at a time so we can enjoy the whole of it together. Jesus is our margin. A life focused on him brings everything into focus. A life with little margin leaves little time with him.

Bringing margin into your life may require repenting. If you're like me, you will probably have to give up something. You will have to say no to someone, to not meet someone's expectations. You will have to say no to the hurried life you have adopted and adapted to. Yes, it may be painful, but the alternative is far more so.

I e-mailed my son in Afghanistan, telling him about my brush with mortality. He replied, saying, "Trust me, there is no reason to be stressed-out in America. You have it all. Just sit back, relax, and enjoy the ride, especially the bumpy parts." I think that is great wisdom from a kid serving on the front lines of the War on Terror and who is nothing less than a hero to me.

Likewise, we have no reason to be stressed-out as followers of Jesus. We have it all—in Jesus we have his spirit, love, wisdom, power, and grace. We have everything we need. Often what we lack is slowing down in order to meet him and accept his power and provision.

Following Jesus' Example

Why is this important? Because we don't meet Jesus in the busyness of life: We meet him in the quietness of life. This is the Jesus way. Don't miss it.

"Very early in the morning, while it was still dark, Jesus got up, left the house and went off to a solitary place, where he prayed" (Mark 1:35). Jesus knew the only way to keep his life on mission was to spend time with his Father.

The same is true for us. The only way we can keep from being consumed by religion is to spend regular time with Jesus. Jesus is the cure for religion. As we grow in intimacy with him, we become more familiar with his ways, we hear his voice more easily, his activity becomes more apparent, and we are more at home with his Spirit. Time with Jesus, freeing us from the clutter and demands of each day, can be the first step to living like Jesus, loving like Jesus, and leaving what Jesus left behind.

Why? We meet Jesus in the margins of life, but it doesn't end there. We also meet the sick, the blind, the poor, and the needy in the margins. It is in the margins of life I meet my own family. I develop all my relationships in the margin. In the margin I have coffee with my wife. It's in the margin that I read God's Word and I hear his voice. It is in my margin that I sense the Spirit drawing close to me, encouraging, convicting, leading me to repent. It's in the margin that most of my opportunities to live, love, and leave take place.

Looking for margin is the Jesus way. Look at Jesus' life, his tempo, his rhythm, and his pace. He was always fully engaged in the moment. He caught things others didn't. He knew when a woman touched him in a crowd. He noticed the tree that didn't bear fruit. He sensed when his disciples were at each other. Jesus moved across the landscape in a certain way. He was always on purpose, but in his movement and pace, he took time to have margins. Likewise, we must look for and move to the margins. We must practice the discipline of slowing. Go ahead—walk across the office. Pay attention to those around. Take your time when you get home. Take your time getting out of your car. Notice your neighbors around you. Try something new. Get in the long line at the grocery store and the tollbooth. Use it as an opportunity to connect—to others and to God. Listen to what is going on in the lives of others in the same line. Pray for those in front of you and those behind you. Pay attention to the clerk. Pause outside your daughter's room; ignore the mess. Listen to what she has to say.

Life is lived in the margins.

DAY 8: FINDING THE JESUS WAY

1. When it comes to living with margin, how would you describe your life?
2. Why is it important that we live with margin as followers of Jesus?
3. What does slowing, abiding, and spending time with Jesus look like for you? What do you want it to look like?

Thoughts, Prayers, and Doodles on the Jesus Way

_____

_____

_____

_____

_____

_____

_____

_____

_____

_____

_____

_____

_____

_____

_____

_____

_____

_____

_____

_____

_____

_____

_____

_____

CHAPTER 9

Control . . . Can I Really Trust You?

*But seek first his kingdom and his righteousness, and all these
things will be given to you as well.*
—Matthew 6:33

> **Toxic Faith:** Living for God protects me from bad
> things.
>
> **The Jesus Way:** Following Jesus means he
> will be with me, bringing good out of every
> circumstance I face. He can be trusted.

I stood in a beautiful garden setting in one of the plantations on
Hilton Head Island. Spring was in full bloom. Azaleas and twisted
oak trees draped with moss filled the landscape. My wife and
children were with me, frozen in what should have been a perfect
moment under other circumstances. My children, then five and two

years old, gripped my hands. Or maybe I gripped theirs. I was overcome with sadness as I gazed down into the open grave at my two-year-old nephew's tiny casket. I wanted to crumble under the grief and the pain, fighting to keep my composure in front of my children as they said good-bye to their little cousin, Victor. They dropped lavender-bloomed azalea branches into the grave as I summoned all my strength to hold back tears. It tore me apart to see my sister and brother-in-law greet the guests warmly and affectionately, and I knew it would only continue to get more difficult for all of us as we moved away from this surreal setting.

Assaulted by Doubts

Not long afterward, I was assaulted by my doubts. Could I trust God any longer? Could I trust him with my children? Why did he allow my innocent young nephew to die so suddenly? Was there something we should have done or not done to prevent it? Did he care about the heartbreak our family was experiencing?

Less than a week earlier, I was visiting my sister's new home. When I left that Friday, Victor had been sitting at the kitchen sink with the spray nozzle pointed at me. He smiled as he shot the water across the room. The next day we were to celebrate his second birthday, healthy, happy, and with everything going right for their family.

But it all came apart.

It began with Victor's sudden illness, followed by multiple wrong diagnoses.

It continued with an ambulance ride to the emergency room.

Then, a grim-faced doctor saying, "I'm sorry."

Learning to Let Go

I left the island a few days later, making a silent vow to myself that I would do everything within my power to protect my children. I was admittedly prone to control, but this was a new level even for me. I determined to protect myself, my family, and my children at all costs.

I have spent most of my life in bondage to control. And it's not that control is inherently bad—self-control and the Spirit's control are vitally important to the Christian life. The Spirit's control is Jesus in us. It is the Jesus way. Yet control packs a lethal punch when it becomes a substitute for trusting God. Let's face it—it's hard to follow when you have to be in control.

The tendency to control is especially dangerous to someone as religious as I have been. When others don't live up to my moral standards, I want to impose restrictions and guidelines so that they can be taught and changed. In fact, the more I love people, the more I find myself wanting to control them. I convince myself that it's for *their* benefit, but often that love grows dim. Those who are closest to me move further away.

The Big One

I don't think I'm the only one who has allowed control to keep me from experiencing the joy and freedom that Jesus offers. As his followers, we know that our need to control first reared its ugly head in another garden that takes center stage in the story of redemption. The characters have changed, and maybe the circumstances have changed, but the drama is the same. Adam and Eve took the fruit and ate it because the serpent convinced them that doing so would give them control over their own destiny (see Gen. 3:5). They began to wonder if perhaps God was holding out on them, that they might need to take some measure of their lives into their own hands.

It's no wonder we are prone to want to control our lives and circumstances. I would go so far as to say control is the major sin in my life and the root of all my religion. However, upon rereading the Gospels, Jesus invites us into a life free of our need to control, inviting us to release ourselves to his care: "Therefore I tell you, do not worry about your life, what you will eat or drink; or about your body, what you will wear. Is not life more important than food, and the body more important than clothes?" (Matt. 6:25). He continues by pointing out how our heavenly Father takes care of the birds, reminding us that we are more important than they are. Following this he points out how futile worry is. It changes absolutely nothing. Then Jesus wraps it up by giving us a whole new way of living that frees us from the need to control. "But seek first his kingdom and his righteousness, and all these things will be given to you as well. Therefore do not worry about tomorrow, for tomorrow will worry about itself. Each day has enough trouble of its own" (Matt. 6:33–34).

Awestruck as I read, I realized that Jesus invites me into a way of life that is about living in the moment. Many of us live in the past, and so often the past is filled with regrets that rob us of the peace of Jesus' presence in our lives. Others of us live in the future where we can anticipate and control our destinies. The only problem is at the end of the day, we discover that we only *thought* we were in control. But Jesus invites us into his presence. He never promised that life would be free of pain and difficulties, but he does invite us into his presence in this life. He is always honest with us—even when life stinks. But he does invite us into a journey, a whole new way of life in which he is with us—always leading, guiding, prodding, loving, consoling, caring, and enduring.

Living in the Moment

When I read the words of Jesus in Matthew, I grieve for my previous misunderstanding. I was encouraged by my desire to obey but broken by the knowledge of the years I spent trying to control the past and the future. Yet my brokenness prepared my heart for healing. Deep from within me I began to weep. Years of doubt and my need for control broke free from deep within my soul. The pain I felt was a healing pain. The truth that hurt was also the truth that healed. God was doing something new in the deepest recesses of my soul. Jesus saw right through me—"O you of little faith." Exactly. My need to control had overwhelmed my faith, because you can't surrender to Jesus when you're trying to control him. All my life I thought I was being supremely religious by managing things on earth to the benefit of God. He needed me, right? With these words from Matthew, Jesus reminded me that I was the one in need.

The day these words became real to me, I experienced the healing of his Spirit in this area of my life. This is the power of the Word of God. In the Gospels, we see Jesus' words heal the sick, give sight to the blind, and raise the dead. His words hold no less power today as they heal our sin-sick lives, give sight to our blind hearts, and raise our dead spirits.

I still fight the desire to control, but it's not the overwhelming need it once was. Daily I find myself dying to my desire to control and living a little more as I rest in Jesus' care. As a result, my relationships are expanding and the depth of intimacy with those I love the most is growing, especially my intimacy with Jesus. The fear that used to come with worrying about the future and trying to control every potential bad thing has been replaced with the joy of living in the moment with Jesus. I lay my head down at night and find rest. In the morning I find my life filled with possibilities, and those burdens that only God is big enough to carry are placed in God's rightful hands.

Even so, as Jesus himself said, "Each day has enough trouble of its own." My son is awaiting another deployment. My daughter's new boyfriend is a Marine, also waiting to be deployed. I pray daily for peace on earth and an end to war. I can't know what the future holds, but I choose to live in this moment. What I do know is that today my son and I will cruise the north Georgia mountains on our motorcycles. We will breathe in the air as we round the sharp curves. We will stop at a small diner and enjoy a meal together. The fall leaves will take our breath away. We will celebrate the life that God has given us together.

I know, in reality, my desire to control will resurface when he deploys. We will find a private place to say good-bye, where I will read a letter I've written to him. We will embrace and weep together. Then he will leave, and I know that Jesus will be with us through all of this.

A life of surrender is a life lived the Jesus way—simply, humbly, and freely walking in the light of truth day by day. A life lived in the moment opens up the portals of heaven and gives us a glimpse of eternity.

Letting go is the Jesus way. You can trust Jesus.

DAY 9: FINDING THE JESUS WAY

1. How does the need to control impact how you follow Jesus?
2. What areas of control do you need to surrender?
3. How can following Jesus in the moment free you from the need to control?
4. What experiences have impacted your life and your ability to let Jesus care for you?

Thoughts, Prayers, and Doodles on the Jesus Way

BOOK TWO

Loving Like Jesus Loves

Loving like Jesus is a divine endeavor that can happen only through the power of Jesus' Spirit within us. This kind of love exceeds human wisdom and takes on a totally impractical expression. When God sent his Son Jesus to die on a cross, so we could enter into a new relationship with him, he showed us the ultimate example of this love. Jesus paid for our sin-debt in full. Love always costs something.

CHAPTER 10

Cup . . . Do I Really Have to Drink All of It?

"Not my will, but yours be done."

—Luke 22:42

> **Toxic Religion:** It's my responsibility to love to the very best of my ability.
>
> **The Jesus Way:** It's not my love, but Jesus' love through me.

It had been building for weeks. Mark played football at the local university and served the church I pastored in the student ministry. Jon was a member of our new church and one of Mark's football coaches. We were watching a *Rocky* movie in our family room when it first started getting out of hand. I don't remember if he challenged me or if I challenged him, but the challenge was on. Surprisingly we were fairly evenly matched. I think God was on my side. What began as a friendly arm-wrestling contest, quickly got out of hand. We had had several private matches that had ended up in a draw, near defeat, and a big misunderstanding. Word had gotten out. I don't think Jon helped. Eventually there was the ultimate challenge. We would go public. We would have a final match on the university campus to settle the score. The winner would humiliate the other by shaving the loser's head (back then I had hair). I told you it was getting out of hand.

The day finally arrived for the big match. I was the underdog. I knew it and felt the building pressure. I remember looking in the mirror that morning thinking, *I'm going to lose my hair.* Baldness wasn't in vogue back in that day. I felt the heat. I ran into some volunteers in the church. They just looked at me, nodding their heads. I knew what it meant. I was in trouble. Now I really felt the pressure! How could I have gotten in this mess? Later that day I went to the university for lunch. Maybe I could find a way out. There were flyers all over campus promoting the match. It was the campus buzz. Everywhere I went people taunted me. I was an idiot. In just a few hours I would square off against a well-conditioned athlete. I didn't have a prayer. There was a price to pay and I had to pay it.

Later that night I was back on campus. It was time. There was no turning back. I entered a room full of electricity and excitement. It looked as if the whole campus had showed up for my certain defeat. Everywhere I turned I saw members of the football team. They were there to pull for one of their own. That's right; they were all there to see me crushed. The lights flashed, the music cranked to full volume with "Eye of the Tiger." I felt as if I was at a WWE event on center stage. In came Mark with his entourage.

I felt alone!

He was amped!

I was scared!

He had a towel over his head like a cage fighter.

I felt trapped in a cage.

Coach Jon wasn't far behind, giving me a taunting look and waving the clippers at me. The moment of truth had come. I felt the pressure. There was no way out.

As we squared off, taking our proper positions, I could smell the adrenaline oozing through Mark's veins. He was hyped up. I can still see the veins popping up along the side of his neck. He looked like a steed ready to lead a herd of wild horses into battle. He was ready for the big game. All of his energy and emotion was channeled into this one moment. This was the big game for him, and he came prepared to win it. No mercy or grace. This would be a moment of truth for me. For a moment he seemed superhuman. I was overwhelmed.

We squared off. Coach Jon gave us our final instructions. I watched nervously as if I were a spectator at my own execution while Mark paced back and forth. It was sort of an out-of-body experience. Coach Jon brought us together. We gripped each other, locking our hands and thumbs together. We placed our elbows on the table. By now Mark was breathing so hard I was getting doused in his spit. A millisecond before we were given the signal to begin,

I pulled back. It was a ploy. It was all I had! I saw an opening. All of the raw pent-up emotion exploded out of Mark's body with a scream that filled the room. We reengaged. Mark looked distracted. We locked together, arm and arm. Mark still looked distracted. The ref slammed his hand on the table signaling the start of the match. My timing was impeccable. I twisted his overinflated bicep toward me with all I had, pulling it into my body. I slammed all of my strength and weight into him using my shoulder. In one single motion his arm slammed against the table. No sooner had the match began, than it was over. Somehow I had done the impossible. Not only had I defeated Mark, I had defeated him in less than a second. It was a good day for preachers everywhere. I kept my hair. Mark looked good with no hair. He looked a lot like The Rock.

Later that night I visited Mark in his dorm room. He was in tears. It was a great night for all. Well, almost all.

I tell this story because I will never forget the pressure I had that particular morning when I woke up. For some strange reason I thought of Jesus in the garden of Gethsemane. I know there is really no comparison, but at the same time, have you ever had to face something inevitable that you knew was going to cost you dearly? Have you ever desperately wanted to find a way out? That's how I felt about my hair and my pride that morning. Without knowing the outcome, I would have avoided what seemed like a certain outcome.

Jesus refused to turn back. He knew that loving us would cost him deeply. The reality of the moment leading up to the cross came crashing in on him in the garden. He longed for a way out, but there was too much at stake. The way of love led him to extreme sacrifice and self-abandonment.

Living like Jesus always leads to loving like Jesus. Loving like Jesus sooner or later leads us to the garden of decision where we, too, must choose to turn back or go all the way, in spite of the outcome. Religion draws a line in the sand and says enough is enough. The Jesus way leads us to that moment when and where we must choose to live and love impractically. Jesus' love is like nothing else.

I feel so weak when it comes to loving like Jesus. I feel I am about to lose my hair. God challenges us to take love to a whole new level. It would be so easy to keep love at an acceptable minimum, but loving like Jesus changes everything.

The good news is it's not my life, nor is it my love. I can't live and love like Jesus. I will always fall short. It is his life lived in and through me. It is his love flowing in and through me. It's not my will, but his. It's not my power, but his. It's not my love, but his.

I struggle here. I must come to surrender. I must enter my garden and experience his life. I'm not alone.

I recently had a conversation with another follower of Jesus from a country where Christianity is illegal; her child had been taken from her. She had not seen her little girl in five years. As she stood before the judge, he told her that all she had to do was deny her faith and her daughter would be returned to her. This was her garden. She refused to deny Christ. The judge was true to his word.

A Different Kind of Love

As I read and reread the Gospels, I can't figure out God's love. My practical mind is overwhelmed by the extreme, disproportionate nature of his love. Francis Chan called it *Crazy Love*[2] in his book, and that's the perfect name for it. It makes no logical sense to love one's enemies, to love the unlovable, to love your enemies so much you are willing to die on a cross. But that's exactly what Jesus did, and he invites us into his way. It may cost us—as it certainly cost Jesus—but it is the very way of love. There is no substitute for loving like Jesus.

One of the most challenging aspects of loving the way Jesus loved is that it demands action. Like the Pharisees, I often find it easier to talk, preach, teach, and write about love than to live it. I can talk the talk, no problem, but that's not enough. The good news is that Jesus' kind of love is life giving. It rids me of all kinds of religion, the mindless activity that sucks the very life out of me. Jesus' love takes me to new depths of surrender and new heights of experience, backing me into corners where only faith can lead me out.

It forces me to continue to pray, *Jesus, show me your way.* I can't love like Jesus loved of my own power, and I need him to be gentle with me, patient with me, helping me in the weakest areas of my life. I need him to transform my heart so that I might experience his presence and transforming power in my family, my network, my community, and my world. Jesus prayed in the garden, "Not my will, but yours be done," reminding us that this kind of practical love doesn't come easy, not even to the Savior of the world. Likewise, when it comes to this kind of love, it's not going to be easy. I can't do it on my own. I will falter and wimp out. I must pray, *Not my love, but yours be done.* I don't have the power to love as Jesus loved, but just as God exerted his will through Jesus, I pray that my surrender will allow him to love through me. This is where the rubber meets the road. By nature this love is not a concept; it is something we do.

Nevertheless, it is a challenging lesson to learn, but more importantly, to live. Jesus demonstrated this love throughout his earthly life, and at no time more than in the hours surrounding his death. On the night before he would be executed, he gathered his closest friends for the Passover meal and what would come to be known as the Last Supper. He humbled himself by washing the feet of his disciples, already aware that Peter would deny him, that Judas had set his plan of betrayal into motion, and that most of the remaining disciples would abandon him at his time of greatest need. Even so, Jesus wanted to spend his last moments with these dearly loved friends.

It's a Costly Kind of Love

In the Gethsemane garden, he asks Peter, James, and John to do nothing more than pray. With his three closest friends at his side, he becomes even more vulnerable and leaves them so he may pray alone. He is deeply troubled and sorrowful in the darkest hours of his time on earth, knowing there is no other way but to surrender to this violent death. Yet, as he pulls himself up, he sees that his disciples— the closest friends he has on earth—are asleep. They don't feel the weight of the moment, and over and over they fail him as they can't stay awake long enough to pray. Even so, Jesus presses on in his love. He wakes his disciples and announces, "Here comes my betrayer," and, fittingly, ironically, Jesus is betrayed with a kiss—an expression of love (see Matt. 26:46–49).

With every lash of the whip, every cane to the face, every puncture wound from the crown of thorns, and the nails through his hands and feet—Jesus loved us. It's easy to miss. It's easy to take for granted, because dying on the cross is part of Jesus' job description. He's the Savior; he has to be the sacrifice to pay for our sin, our rebellion. Yet he was fully man, and as such he had the same free will that God has given us. He could have stopped at any point, calling ten thousand angels to his aid. But he didn't. Instead he pressed into the love of God and prayed, "Not my will but yours."

Loving like Jesus is the ultimate expression of love—there is truly no greater love. He loved through the darkness and loneliness of being betrayed by his own creation, and he loved through the hurt that came with seeing his followers fail him. Loving like Jesus is a challenge because it always involves death—death to your pride, death to your bitterness, death to your overly religious ways. It always comes with a struggle, and it always involves surrender. Loving like Jesus is impossible of our own accord. Our only hope is to allow Jesus to love through us.

This involves the same kind of death Jesus experienced in Gethsemane. It requires a death to my preferences, my desires, my preferred path, my way, my emotions, and my will. Like Jesus, it takes time in the garden alone with God. It takes us coming to the end of ourselves. It requires that Jesus takes over where we end. Yes, this becomes the place where he begins. It's not my love, but it is his love through me. *Dear Father, turn my prayers into actions.*

DAY 10: FINDING THE JESUS WAY

1. Reflect on a time in your life when human love just wasn't enough.
2. How can God's Spirit enable you to love like Jesus?
3. What does your Gethsemane look like?
4. Take a moment and surrender your life once again to Jesus and his way. Invite him to love through you.

Thoughts, Prayers, and Doodles on the Jesus Way

_____

_____

_____

_____

_____

_____

_____

_____

_____

_____

CHAPTER 11

Perfume . . . Was It a Waste?

"Why are you bothering this woman?
She has done a beautiful thing to me."
—Matthew 26:10

Toxic Religion: Love is always practical and makes sense.

The Jesus Way: Jesus' love is impractical and costly.

ords like *unconditional, extreme, perfect, crazy,* and *absolute* have all been used to describe the special kind of love Jesus lived out, but one other word has become part of my experience. Jesus' love is *impractical.* For a very practically minded man, this is a big deal. If you don't believe me, take a look at the way of Jesus when it comes to love. Listen to what he said and watch the way he lived. Why would any rational person want to love his enemies?

What can it possibly gain us to pray for those who persecute us? Jesus knew, and he demonstrated it to us. Of course, this impracticality makes sense when I am on the receiving end; it's when I'm to exhibit this ridiculous love that I start to hesitate. This kind of love requires a rethinking of everything we know about life.

As I shared earlier, for me this rethinking came on the heels of a nearly fatal experience with my wife. She encountered a car—or might I say, a car encountered her—one evening when we were out jogging in our neighborhood. After her accident, a week in the hospital, surgery reconstructing her leg, and months of recovery and rehabilitation, I decided something special was in order for our upcoming twenty-fifth wedding anniversary. I was nineteen when I proposed to Tami, and I bought her a ring with the budget of a nineteen-year-old. She has always loved it, but as I contemplated our anniversary and my growing love for her, I wanted her to have something that cost me, something that showed my love for her. A new ring sounded perfect.

I began doing research as I prepared to find the perfect diamond. While I wanted it to be special, my key criterion was finding the right price. I love her, and I wanted to do something extraordinary, but I was also committed to sound judgment and practicality. A few days into my search, a young woman who seemed to be as excited as I was about finding the right ring for Tami greeted me at a jewelry store. As I told her my story, she smiled brightly and said, "I have the perfect diamond for you." She was right. It was a flawless, square-cut diamond that sparkled beyond my wildest imagination. By that, I mean it was priced far beyond my budget. Disappointed, I asked her if she had anything else. She did, and they were all beautiful, but they just weren't the same. I explained my dilemma to her, and she seemed to understand. As I left, she smiled and said, "It will be here if you want to reconsider."

For the next few weeks I drove all across Atlanta, looking for the perfect ring to give my wife, but I couldn't get the first diamond off my mind. Finally I returned to that first jewelry store, and the same young woman greeted me. She smiled a knowing smile and said, "Let me go get that diamond." This time, we placed the perfect stone in the perfect setting, which only served to increase its cost. Once again I left the store discouraged by my need to be practical, not knowing if I would ever find the right ring.

One Sunday morning during a worship service, God seemed to be nudging me especially hard. I was engaged in the pastor's message, but before long I started thinking about that diamond. I began to dream about what it would cost to express this kind of love to Tami, to give her the gift I truly wanted to give. I thought about the sacrifice I would have to make over the next months to make this expression of love a reality—I would take my lunch rather than going out; I could sell some of the clutter in my garage and basement; I would take advantage of extra speaking and writing opportunities, as well as apply my Christmas bonus to the purchase. I began to dream creatively about how I could come up with the money to place this ring on Tami's finger, even going so far as to imagine this expression of love being passed down to my daughter and, one day, to her daughter.

Pondering this, I found myself thinking about a passage of Scripture found in Matthew 26:6–13:

> While Jesus was in Bethany in the home of a man known as Simon the Leper, a woman came to him with an alabaster jar of very expensive perfume, which she poured on his head as he was reclining at the table. When the disciples saw this, they were indignant. "Why this waste?" they asked. "This perfume could have been sold at a high price and the money given to the poor." Aware of this, Jesus said to them, "Why are you bothering this woman? She has done a beautiful thing to me. The poor you will always have with you, but you will not always have me. When she poured this perfume on my body, she did it to prepare me for burial. I tell you the truth, wherever this gospel is preached throughout the world, what she has done will also be told, in memory of her."

I was struck by the nature of this passage—what is more impractical than this woman's demonstration of love toward Jesus? The disciples protested the wasting of such an expensive resource, wondering why she didn't express her love for Jesus in another way. No one would have questioned her had she run into the streets, telling anyone who came near about her Lord, Jesus. She might have given him food to eat or offered him a place to stay or given a more reasonable gift. Yet something motivated her to pour her expensive perfume on Jesus' head, ceremonially foreshadowing his death and burial. What a waste, the disciples thought.

"Why don't you do something *practical* with your money?" the disciples might have asked. They failed to realize that the most practical thing this woman could do was something totally impractical, and that's what she did. Here lies a root of the disciples' religious ways: To the overly religious, love is measured, sensible, and understandable. But to love the Jesus way, loving as he loved, is to love wildly, outrageously, with no regard for the cost. Loving as Jesus loved doesn't make sense.

On Monday morning I went back to the jewelry store where the same young woman met me and asked, "Are you ready?"

I smiled and said, "I am."

With diamond in hand, I now had the responsibility to give it to Tami. Now I was on a roll. I thought about Paris. I thought about the top of the Empire State Building. I thought of a romantic evening in downtown Atlanta, not very far from our home. I thought about a starry night overlooking a moonlit ocean. Then it hit me. I had the perfect place for my totally impractical gift—our patio.

Tami arrived home on Friday evening from a rather difficult trip when she had buried her dear grandmother. I invited her back to the patio that was enclosed by a garden we had created with our own hands. She sat on the swing my children gave her for Mother's Day ten years earlier. In that simple setting I started at the beginning of our life together and told her how much I loved her. It wasn't long until we both were crying uncontrollably. It was a perfect moment.

Then I reached down to where I had hidden the ring. I took it out of the box and placed it on her finger. I couldn't imagine giving her this totally impractical gift any other way. It was beautiful.

Today, every time I see it on Tami's hand I am reminded of how much I love her, but more importantly, how much Jesus loves us. I don't want to overspiritualize the purchase, or even to imply that we should all spend extravagantly to show love to others, but through this experience I understood in a new way what it means to love as Jesus loved. I've come to realize that God's love for us and through us is a precious gift that can never be explained in practical terms. Religion puts this love in a box, but Jesus took his love out of the box and placed it on a cross, just outside a garden where he had struggled so mightily.

DAY 11: FINDING THE JESUS WAY

1. How is Jesus' love impractical?
2. How can being practical limit the way you love?
3. Describe a time in your life when you loved impractically.
4. What does loving impractically look like in your life right now?

Thoughts, Prayers, and Doodles on the Jesus Way

CHAPTER 12

Sinners . . . How Do I Know God Loves Me?

But God demonstrates his own love for us in this:
While we were still sinners, Christ died for us.
—Romans 5:8

Toxic Religion: God loves me only when I'm lovable.

The Jesus Way: Jesus loves me in my worst moment.

knew I needed to see a doctor, but I was hesitant to make the appointment. My regular doctor had no openings, so I reluctantly made an appointment with his young new partner. Upon arriving, I was taken to the examination room where the nurse performed her requisite blood pressure screening. The young doctor came in shortly and sat across from me, asking about my symptoms. After I gave him the full rundown, he left and stayed away for a few minutes. He returned, announcing his diagnosis before he had even taken the time to examine me. The diagnosis sounded like something he had come up with by typing my symptoms into WebMD. I suggested an alternate diagnosis based on my own research and experience, but he assured me of his initial decision and wrote a prescription, sending me on my way. Severely disappointed with the visit, I decided I was done with him. I went out of my way to make sure I didn't see this doctor again, even to the point of waiting weeks to see another physician in a different practice.

My Love Language

Things were going well until I landed in the hospital a few months later (see chapter 8). My blood pressure had spiked, causing severe headaches and chest pain, and I finally submitted to the emergency room. The next morning as I lay waiting cardiac tests, the doctor arrived. As he walked into the room, I contemplated running for the door before I remembered I was wearing a backless hospital gown. It was the WebMD doctor.

He asked me what was going on, and I began to list my symptoms for him. He immediately transitioned the conversation by saying, "I understand you're going through a lot. Isn't your son serving in Afghanistan?"

How did he know that? He was now speaking a language that communicated to me he really cared, and I lowered my defenses somewhat. We talked about my son for a few moments, and he asked me if there was anything else. With my walls lowering even more,

I replied, "Well, there's Sam." Sam was my daughter's boyfriend who recently died during a procedure to remove a cancerous mass in his chest. As I tried to explain Sam's story, I began to fall apart. Understanding, the young new doctor put his hand on my shoulder and began to console me.

That morning my WebMD doctor loved me well. Before that experience I had vowed that I would never see him again. I did everything I could to avoid him. If I hadn't ended up in the hospital and if he hadn't been on call, I'm sure I would have lived up to my word. However, that morning he became my doctor. He loved me well, and loving me well, I was now able to love him in return.

God knows that for us to love him well, we must be loved well by him. And does he love us well! It doesn't stop there—when we are loved well by him and we love him well in return, we are able to love others well.

How does God love us well? He tells us of his love over and over again, and he shows us through his Son.

God Says It

Maybe you remember saying "I love you" to a girlfriend or boyfriend for the first time. It's not something you take lightly, nor is it something you do too early. "Hey, great evening . . . I had a good time (little peck on the cheek). By the way, I love you." It doesn't work that way, and on top of being totally inappropriate, it would be sort of weird.

First, you fly a few test balloons: "I really like you. No, I mean I really like you a lot. Like, more than like. I just love your hair. I love your smile. I love the sound of your voice." Finally you plan for it . . . flowers . . . dinner . . . the rehearsed conversation . . . and you say it. Maybe slowly, gauging the reaction, or maybe all at once, so you can say it before you lose your nerve. "I love you." And when the object of your affection almost cuts you off saying, "I love you too!" it changes everything. You are no longer available. You are taken. You are loved.

Now, on the other hand, if you finally work up the nerve to say "I love you" for the first time and your love replies with, "I think you're sweet" or something like that, you are in real trouble. You better have a backup plan like, "Just kidding!"

The good news is that when God says, "I love you," you can count on it. God tells us he loves us over and over again: "I've never quit loving you and never will" (Jer. 31:3 *The Message*). Speaking to his disciples, Jesus put it this way: "I have loved you" (NLT).

When our son was in Afghanistan, one of the primary ways he communicated was via e-mail. Every day Tami and I opened our e-mail accounts, hoping for a message. Because of the nature of his job there were times we would go four and five weeks with no word from him, but always, eventually, he would write. We skimmed it first, praying not to hear of an explosion or accident or casualty. Then, we read it again, slower, digesting his words and understanding his meaning. We continued to read the messages again the next day, and the next, and over and over until we heard from him again.

The Scriptures are God's e-mails to us, his personal notes to you and to me. Yet religion has overwhelmed us to the point of intimidation. We shy away from the Bible, avoiding it out of guilt. We fail to realize the Bible isn't a rule book designed to create some kind of moral code, nor is it a guidebook for religious culture. The Scriptures are God's love letters to you and me. His purpose for giving us his Scripture is to reveal himself to us, letting us know just how much he loves us and showing us a better way, his way, the way of Jesus.

God Shows Us

And just to be sure we don't miss it, God not only says he loves us, but he shows us that he loves us through his people, even at our worst moments. I will never forget calling my dad after I left his home. I was very much like the Prodigal Son, taking all I had and leaving home for a life of open rebellion, drugs, and alcohol. Like the prodigal, I ultimately came to my senses, and I still remember the conversation I had with my dad. Over a pay phone line crackling with static, I asked him if I could come home and try to get my life together. It was my worst moment of the most profound humility. I had hit bottom and was broke, unemployed, and strung out. I expected, "You can come home if. . . ." But instead, I heard my dad say, "Come home and know that nothing you have done will ever be mentioned here again." In my worst moment, God loved me well through my dad. I can still remember the extra effort and the excitement that came with him getting ready for my return.

It didn't stop there. God loved me well through Frank. When I returned home and went to look for employment, Frank gave me a job handling his money. I thought he had lost his mind, but he knew exactly what he was doing as he demonstrated God's love for me.

Meanwhile every Monday night at church, AC met with some boys from my rough neighborhood to love them as Jesus would. I will never forget the day he came to me and said, "God has laid you on my heart. Would you be willing to come over on Monday night and help me out with the guys?" At the time I was working for Frank, attending worship services out of respect for my dad, and only drinking and doing drugs on the weekend, but I was far from clean. Yet I remember thinking that if God really did speak to AC about my helping, then maybe God wasn't finished with me. Before this I really felt that maybe I had crossed some religious line and gone too far in my sin. I was afraid God had moved on and would never forgive or accept me.

Later God showed me his love through Travis, a pastor friend of my dad's who preached at a revival service in our town when Tami and I were just beginning to consider Jesus and his ways. Travis came to see me during the week, inviting me to go to the revival meeting. He said, "David, you are special. God loves you and has something very important he wants to do in and through your life." Intrigued, I went to those services where I ultimately made the most important decision of my life—to follow Jesus.

At the same time and during the whole time, there was Mom. She also asked Tami and me to go to the revival meeting, and there was something about her tender invitation that captured me. I responded simply in the affirmative, and Tami and I attended with her.

Granny was Tami's grandmother and a devoted follower of Jesus. God loved Tami and me both through Granny. She went to that same revival my mom invited us to, where Travis was the visiting pastor, where AC worked with the rough boys, where Frank attended, and where my dad served as pastor. Granny prayed for me. After I had walked out the church door, cursing Christianity and the church, declaring that I would never return, Granny simply prayed.

God used these people to come together at the right time in my life, under the right circumstances, to show me how much he loved me. There was nothing artificial about this love, nothing prefabricated or by the book. When religion consumes us, we implement the law and pretend it is love. My parents could have thrown a Bible at me, telling me to get my life straight before God. Judging by my track record at the time, Frank should have never given me any responsibility, least of all over his money. Granny could have called me a blasphemer. Yet all of these people—and countless others in my life—embraced not religion but Jesus. In doing so, they loved me well, showing me the Jesus way by allowing him to love me through them.

Jesus reminds us that those who are forgiven most love him the most:

> "Two men owed money to a certain moneylender. One
> owed him five hundred denarii, and the other fifty. Neither
> of them had the money to pay him back, so he canceled
> the debts of both. Now which of them will love him

more?" Simon replied, "I suppose the one who had the
bigger debt canceled." "You have judged correctly."
(Luke 7:41–43)

I believe my life is proof of that, and I am committed to loving others well in return, but this would have never been possible if
I wasn't first loved well. We love well only when we understand and
experience his love well.

DAY 12: FINDING THE JESUS WAY

1. How has God loved you well? List the two or three
   instances that have impacted you the most.
2. Reflect on the people God has put in your life who have
   loved you well. Make a list of them, noting how they loved
   you, and thank God for them.
3. Invite God to show you how he is trying to love someone
   through you.

Thoughts, Prayers, and Doodles on the Jesus Way

_____

_____

_____

_____

CHAPTER 13

Enemies . . . What's Wrong with an Eye for an Eye?

*"You have heard that it was said, 'Love your neighbor
and hate your enemy.' But I tell you: Love your enemies
and pray for those who persecute you."*
—Matthew 5:43–44

> **Toxic Religion:** We love only those who are like us and easy to love.
>
> **The Jesus Way:** Jesus invites us into a whole new way that includes loving our enemies.

I had known him for only a few minutes, but we were already friends. We were certainly brothers, both of us with a passion for Jesus and his ways. He is a Middle Easterner, and he heads up the US side of a ministry, training house-church pastors and distributing Bibles in his home country. I was in his office and we were on a Skype call (free video-conferencing technology) to communicate with a house-church pastor from one of the most dangerous places in the world to be a follower of Jesus—much less a pastor. He was risking his life to speak with us, and my new friend was obviously concerned for the well-being of the pastor on the other side of the connection. He kept asking the pastor if his line was secured, yet the pastor seemed to have little regard for his own safety, even joking about being at a friend's house. He was obviously more interested in living the Jesus way than maintaining his own safety.

Over the next fifteen or twenty minutes, he told story after story of God's missional activity in his country. It was amazing and over-whelming for me. If God's activity in our world is his invitation to join him, I was getting my invitation. It was loud and clear. I felt as if I had been set up. I knew I would soon have to go. Before this unex-pected conversation I had no idea that the people in that country were so hungry for the gospel. I had heard rumors of God's activity, but until now they had fallen mostly on deaf ears. This was usually the case. "Though seeing, they do not see; though hearing, they do not hear or understand" (Matt. 13:13). Now it was apparent. God had gotten my attention. I saw how hungry and how ready these people were to embrace Jesus and his ways.

The house-church pastor shared his stories of God at work. It was amazing. He told of experience after experience of God's mighty movement in his country. I still couldn't get over how what I thought was one of the most godless countries in the world—one I would consider an enemy to our country, to Christianity, and even to me personally—was experiencing the mighty presence of Jesus. He told of his experience in the university. He presented a paper on the history of Christianity in his Islamic country. Over and over again, the students broke out in applause as the light of the gospel made its way through the archives of history. He told us stories about getting freshly translated copies of the New Testament into the hands of people eager to hear the Good News. He told of one young man he had encountered on a bridge. He had given up hope and was about to jump. His religion had let him down. The house-church pastor pulled over and spoke into his life about the hope of Jesus, talking him off the bridge, giving him a copy of the New Testament, and leaving him to start a new life.

As I listened to story after story, I couldn't help but notice in the background were the five thousand copies of the New Testament that had been smuggled into the country by a former drug smuggler turned Bible smuggler. They were waiting to be distributed to others who are discovering Jesus and his ways.

I felt as if I had gone back in time and landed in an ancient land where religious freedom was nonexistent. I felt compelled to pray, and my new friend invited me to do so. I asked the pastor how I could pray, and he asked me to pray for his country in a time when so many people are turning to Jesus and his ways. The harvest was indeed plentiful, but the laborers are so few. He also asked me to pray for a neighboring country he would soon visit, ignoring his own danger. He seemed to have such little regard for himself. This man truly understood loving like Jesus loves.

When I got off the phone, I asked my friend how we are to respond as followers of Jesus to this Middle Eastern country. Our relationship in this region has been complicated by the ongoing war. His response was simple: "We are to love our enemies."

Love Our Enemies

As I left the conference room, my heart leaped with excitement and my head spun with possibilities. My little religious world was being turned upside down, and images of peace on earth began to dance through my head. Something totally unexpected came over me as I pondered what I thought I knew about this country—my heart began to soften for the people there. Even though the government and elements in this country are supplying explosives intended to kill our American troops, troops like my son, I know that God is up to something there. Even as I write these words, my son's deployment has been moved to a new location bordering this country. I can't help but ask, "What is God up to?" How am I to respond? What I do know is new relationships are being formed. A new vision, Jesus' vision, is emerging in my heart, and a new response began to surface in my mind. I no longer have an excuse for not loving my enemies. The only question left to answer is, how? What does it mean to love your enemies?

My old religious ways tell me to move on, go to church, read a passage, ask God for something I really need. Yet somehow as I move into the ways of Jesus, I know that this isn't enough. I have to go;

I have to help. I have heard the Macedonia call. As a follower of Jesus I have to go. Plans are being made even as I write these words. By the time you read these words, I will have gone at least once with new plans on the horizon. Loving like Jesus loves, loving our enemies, moves us out of our Facebook networks and MySpace friendships into a hostile and challenging world. It brings new light to the world's struggles and instills new hope.

For now, loving my enemies begins with going. It is amazing what happens when we go. I used to try to figure it all out on my own, but I'm beginning to learn that going means simply following him. He will show us the way as we go. Another aspect of losing my religion is that I no longer have to be in control. I no longer have to have an agenda other than to love like Jesus loves. I used to think that God changes the world through our going, but now I am learning that God changes us when we go. He is already changing the world.

When my team goes on this upcoming trip, we will visit those who are following Jesus and his ways. We will pray for them and find ways to encourage them. We will spend time training their pastors. In return, they will train us how to love like Jesus. We will take the money we might normally use to clothe our bodies (often from clothing made in sweatshops in impoverished countries) to buy Bibles for distributing to those who are spiritually hungry. We will forge new relationships, overcoming our fears and prejudices. God will change our hearts, and we will become more like Jesus.

That's just the beginning. We will go back, and when we do, this new love for our enemies will draw us in. We will take greater risks.

We will go deeper. We will get more involved. Our love will be more apparent. Some will even give up their lives in order to go.

Then we will go back again and again. Each time our regard for ourselves will diminish, as our love for our enemies grows stronger and stronger. This love will become our cross and on this cross we will give our lives. This is the Jesus way.

Who Is Our Enemy?

The first and most natural question we ask is, "Who are our enemies?" We don't have to go halfway around the world to find them. The world is filled with enemies. In some ways this is good news—if we as followers of Jesus are more defined by our love for our enemies than our love for our neighbors, we have lots of opportunities for being defined.

Since there is no shortage of enemies in our world, there is no shortage of people to love. Who are our enemies? Are our enemies the militants and terrorists we have come to associate with the Middle East? Are they the political parties we have grown accustomed to voting against? Are they the school systems and teachers who oppose Creationism? Are they those who violate our laws and spend their lives behind bars? Are they the hospitals and doctors who perform procedures that appall us? Are they those who are employed by the sex industries? Are they the poor and less fortunate in many of our rural areas and inner cities? Are they the tattooed and pierced who have come to be associated with a new generation? Are they the

Buddhists, Hindus, Muslims, or those who have their own beliefs? Or maybe my enemy is the guy who beat me for a promotion in my last job or who cut me off on the way to work. When it comes to our enemies, there is no shortage to choose from.

Redemptive Goodwill

You can't follow Jesus and not love your enemies. Jesus has what Martin Luther King Jr., a previous pioneer of love for one's enemy, called a "redemptive goodwill."[3] Peter reached this same conclusion after spending three years with Jesus. While others saw the failure of Jesus to return to Earth quickly as a problem, Peter saw it as Jesus' very nature, saying, "The Lord is not slow in keeping his promise, as some understand slowness. He is patient with you, not wanting anyone to perish, but everyone to come to repentance" (2 Pet. 3:9). Perhaps my favorite expression of Jesus' redemptive goodwill comes from Paul: "But where sin increased, grace increased all the more" (Rom. 5:20).

Costly Love

Loving our enemies always costs. Don't think it doesn't. Jesus tells us, "Blessed are those who are persecuted because of righteousness, for theirs is the kingdom of heaven." Loving our enemies is a form of righteousness and always leads to some kind of persecution. According to Jesus, people will "insult you, persecute you and falsely say all kinds of evil against you" (Matt. 5:10–11).

No More Eye for An Eye

If you don't believe it, just keep reading. Later, in this same sermon, Jesus lays out what this new way of love looks like—including loving our enemies. Once again he begins by showing us a whole new way of living.

> "You have heard that it was said, 'Eye for eye, and tooth for tooth.' But I tell you, do not resist an evil person. If someone strikes you on the right cheek, turn to him the other also. And if someone wants to sue you and take your tunic, let him have your cloak as well. If someone forces you to go one mile, go with him two miles. Give to the one who asks you, and do not turn away from the one who wants to borrow from you." (Matt. 5:38–42)

"Eye for eye, and tooth for tooth" is found in the Torah and was meant to limit retribution. In the words of Gandhi, "An eye for an eye only ends up in making the whole world blind."[4] Jesus came, showing us a whole new way of love that stops violence, extortion, and oppression. By loving our enemies, we remove their power to cause us harm. Thus we have Jesus' teaching on turning the other cheek, offering our tunic, going the extra mile, and giving them what they want. All these actions of love restore our dignity and cause the power of love to overshadow the offense. This is not retribution or passivity but rather what happens when we use our redemptive imagination to love our enemies. This is redemptive goodwill.

Defining Mark

Later Jesus lays out how loving our enemy is our defining mark as his followers:

> "You have heard that it was said, 'Love your neighbor and hate your enemy.' But I tell you: Love your enemies and pray for those who persecute you, that you may be sons of your Father in heaven. He causes his sun to rise on the evil and the good, and sends rain on the righteous and the unrighteous. If you love those who love you, what reward will you get? Are not even the tax collectors doing that? And if you greet only your brothers, what are you doing more than others? Do not even pagans do that? Be perfect, therefore, as your heavenly Father is perfect."
> (Matt. 5:43–48)

This kind of living involves a redemptive imagination that can only happen when we follow Jesus. Our tendency is to isolate and protect ourselves from those things that threaten us. Jesus leads us into the fiery furnace and the lions's den. If we really want to love our enemies, we must start by going to our enemies. As we go, God has a way of transforming our hearts, which is why loving our enemies always begins with ourselves. That's why I've chosen to spend the rest of my life going in and out of the Middle East so Jesus' love may flow through me into the lives of many broken, hurting, and helpless people.

DAY 13: FINDING THE JESUS WAY

1. Who is your enemy? Be specific.
2. How can you show love to that person (or those people) right now, or the next opportunity you have? Be equally specific.

Thoughts, Prayers, and Doodles on the Jesus Way

_____

_____

_____

_____

_____

_____

_____

_____

_____

_____

_____

_____

CHAPTER 14

Friend . . . But I Don't Know Any Sinners

*"It is not the healthy who need a doctor, but the sick.
I have not come to call the righteous, but sinners."*

—Mark 2:17

Toxic Religion: We build religious walls around us to protect ourselves from people who aren't like us.

The Jesus Way: Jesus pushes us outside our walls and comfort zones where we become "friends of sinners."

When I became a follower of Jesus, many well-intended religious people were quick to point out my need to stay away from those "sinners." It wasn't long until I felt the need to start building my own set of religious walls around my life. This was not all bad. At the time I needed a little separation from the things

I had consumed in my former life. I'm convinced that, for me, a time of withdrawal was an important part of living the Jesus way. At the same time you can't live like Jesus, love like Jesus, and leave what Jesus left behind if you don't allow Jesus to love others through you. This is why his love always takes us outside our religious comfort zones and compels us to love those who are far outside our spiritual communities.

Unfortunately we often choose to stay within them, leading to a kind of narcissistic religious consumerism that is all about ourselves. Somehow I can't believe this is what Jesus had in mind for his followers. Perhaps this is the reason I find myself appalled by those who tend to keep their faith to themselves.

The Dignity She Deserved

I couldn't believe my eyes as we rode past a Christian amusement park that attempted to replicate the world Jesus lived in. My friends and I were incredulous at this bastion of religious consumerism and were still talking about it when we stopped for lunch. We were in the city for a ministry conference, and I was glad to be spending time with these friends who were missionaries, pastors, and pastors' wives.

We spied what seemed to be a good opportunity for lunch and walked inside. Upon opening the door of the restaurant, I was immediately taken aback. The women who greeted us were close to my daughter's age and scantily clad. At that moment I didn't know what to do; I was considered to be the spiritual leader of the group, and

I recognized my opportunity to model the Jesus way. However, my autonomic nervous system began to kick in, and all rationale went out the window. I was operating on instinct, fight or flight. What would Jesus do?

We stayed and were quickly seated and attended to by one of the scantily clad waitresses. As we began to talk with her, one of the guys in our party asked if she liked her job. She answered, almost embarrassed, by telling us about some of her dreams. She was enrolled at a local university and studying to become a teacher. She enjoyed children and looked forward to being able to teach them to spell and subtract and find China on a map. I began to realize the other women were probably similar to this one, with dreams, ideas, and plans for their lives, even though they were working in a less-than-ideal environment.

We didn't throw down the four spiritual laws, try to convert her, or condemn her employment. We simply treated her with dignity.

I can't help but wonder what this woman's everyday life was like. Are there difference makers in her life? Are there encouragers? Are there people around her, demonstrating the way Jesus loves her, showing her the way? If not, I pray God would send someone to her, someone to help her discover the simplicity and love of Jesus.

Naked and Ashamed

Reading the Gospels after this encounter, I was still trying to envision what Jesus might have done when I realized that he *was* confronted with a similar situation. In John 8, we are told of Jesus' encounter with the woman caught in adultery and brought to him by the religious leaders. They intended to trap Jesus, thinking they were setting him up in an impossible situation—would he abide by their long-held laws and stone the offensive woman, or would he back down in the "grace" he always talked about and let her off? The religious leaders believed that either way, they won. But Jesus turned the whole scenario around on them, inviting any of them who had led sinless lives to throw the first stone at the woman. All of a sudden the pressure was transferred onto the religious. If they threw their stones, they were claiming to be sinless. On the other hand, if they dropped their stones, they might be admitting their need for grace. Stunning the leaders, Jesus' comments changed the whole tone of the encounter and thinned out the crowd, leaving only him and the adulterous woman. (It takes two to commit adultery, and I'm not sure where the guy was who was caught with her, but he was obviously absent from the encounter.)

It's not a stretch to imagine the woman was standing before Jesus, naked and ashamed; after all, she had been brought to Jesus after being caught in the very act of adultery. Yet Jesus didn't shield his eyes or turn around so he couldn't see her nude body or ask her to come back once she had put some clothes on. In fact, he says nothing at all about her behavior. He inquires only about the religious leaders, who abandoned their condemnation upon seeing that Jesus had turned the tables on them. Jesus tells the woman, "Neither do I condemn you. . . . Go now and leave your life of sin" (John 8:11).

Jesus was the master of multitasking. In one fell swoop, he puts the religious leaders in their place by showing them they, too, needed grace, showed merciful love for the adulterous woman, instructed her in the right way, and taught everyone a lesson. Wow! There is life in that kind of love, the kind that doesn't back down from an uncomfortable situation, the kind that zigs when religion zags. The "religious leaders" (who are very appropriately named, if you ask me) exhibited just that—religion—by condemning both the sin and the sinner, by humiliating her, by rejecting her, and trying to teach her a lesson. Religious people are skilled at keeping sinners away, but here we see Jesus was a friend to sinners and even loved them.

Friend of Sinners

The Gospels refer to Jesus by many different names that reveal his character and his love: Messiah (John 4:25), Savior (Luke 2:11), Son of God (Matt. 27:43), the Word (John 1:1), Lamb of God (John 1:29), Bread of Life (John 6:48), Living Water (John 4:10), Wonderful Counselor, Mighty God, Everlasting Father, Prince of Peace (Isa. 9:6), the Way, the Truth, and the Life (John 14:6) . . . all of these demonstrate his power, his glory, and his greatness. On the other hand, there are other names for Jesus in the Gospels, names that aren't necessarily edifying. The religious crowds were put off by Jesus' unorthodox behavior and often referred to him as a glutton, a drunkard, friend of tax collectors, and even a friend of sinners (Matt. 11:18–20).

"Friend of sinners" is one of my favorites, probably because I am a sinner. I always have been. Yet the good news of the gospel turns hardened sinners into saints by the grace of Jesus' sacrifice. Many people in my life have demonstrated the character of Jesus to me by being a friend of sinners, a friend of *me*. Those of us who follow Jesus' ways, then, can only ask this question: "Who are the sinners in my life, and am I counted among their friends?" This is a question worth spending some time on. In a typical week, do you spend any time at all with people who don't consider themselves Christians? Do you seek out opportunities to befriend people who are living a sinner's lifestyle?

If we are gut-level honest with ourselves, it is not unusual for Christians to build religious walls that keep out those who live differently. We can even use our churches to build these walls— instead of being the church that attracts and embraces sinners, we build church buildings that keep sinners out. We forget that Jesus clearly stated that his house shall be "a house of prayer for all nations" (Mark 11:17). The word *nation* here refers to people groups, which come in all shapes and sizes. It's possible the woman brought to Jesus by the religious leaders in John 8 might have fit into the people group associated with prostitutes or the sex industry.

Loving like Jesus will always bring us into uncomfortable situations. We will be vulnerable and often misunderstood by others. We may be accused of being gluttons and drunkards and friends of sinners. Being friends of sinners may require a change in our behaviors and relationships—it's not going to be easy, but it will be the best way. It's the Jesus way.

DAY 14: FINDING THE JESUS WAY

1. Reflect on how being overly religious has kept you from loving sinners.
2. List the people and places in your life that allow you to be a friend of sinners.

Thoughts, Prayers, and Doodles on the Jesus Way

_____

_____

_____

_____

_____

_____

_____

_____

_____

_____

_____

CHAPTER 15

Samaritan . . . Is He Really My Neighbor?

"Go and do likewise."

—Luke 10:37

> **Toxic Religion:** We cross the street in order to avoid involvement and danger.
>
> **The Jesus Way:** Following Jesus often leads to danger that will cost us something if not everything.

It was 4:00 a.m., and like many decisions made at 4:00 a.m., it was not a smart one. I was headed to work for the UPS morning shift and noticed the only other car on the road was driving erratically alongside me. Glancing over, I saw the driver trying to get my attention, obviously distressed. He sped around me and pulled off into the emergency lane, waving wildly at me. A thousand thoughts ran through my head, not the least of which was for my personal safety.

What if this guy was crazy? Is it my responsibility as a follower of Jesus to put myself in harm's way for the sake of someone else?

I pulled over in the emergency lane ahead of him, leaving my car in gear. I rolled down my window as the stranger approached me, keeping his distance at first. He was lost and asked my help in finding his way. Relieved, I began to give him directions. Yet as I described the last turn to him, he reached through the window and grabbed me. I shoved him as hard as I could, forcing him away from the car and stomping down on the accelerator, adrenaline pumping as I drove away.

I didn't look back or slow down until I got to the UPS loading docks, and I spent the morning trying to escape my experience by presorting packages. After my shift ended, I returned home and told my wife the story. She agreed it was a careless thing to do. I explained that I was just trying to do what Jesus might have done, but it had backfired.

Two days later, again on my way to work at 4:00 a.m., I pulled off the interstate exit ramp and stopped at the traffic light. On the shoulder to my right was a car, the driver with his head under the raised hood (did I mention I was in a bad part of town) and jumper cables attached to the battery, not connected to another battery. I tried to ignore the driver, who was now standing between his car and mine, but our eyes eventually met. I rolled down my window, and he asked if I could give him a jump. Once again, a thousand questions raced through my mind. A preliminary shot of adrenaline went shooting through me as I remembered the similar encounter only two days earlier. I thought, *Is this a test, God? What if it turns out worse than last time? What would Jesus do?*

Convicted, I made a U-turn and lined up my car with the unattached ends of the jumper cable. After connecting them and successfully starting the man's car, I shook his hand and continued on to work without incident. For days I pondered the two experiences, asking myself and God where my responsibility ends as a follower of Jesus. Praying, meditating, and reading the Gospels, I came to the story of the Good Samaritan in Luke 10.

A New Twist on the Torah

In this story Jesus has been asked the all-important question, "What must I do to inherit eternal life?" Jesus, as he was so adept at doing, responds by turning the question around: "How do you read it?" The religious leader, an expert in the Law, gives what we might call the Sunday school answer: "'Love the Lord your God with all your heart and with all your soul and with all your strength and with all your mind'; and, 'Love your neighbor as yourself.'" I'm sure the expert felt a surge of pride; he'd given a great answer, displaying both that he knew the Scriptures and that he understood where Jesus was going with his line of questioning. Religious people often have the Sunday school answers at the ready, prepared at any juncture to show off how well they know the Bible.

But the religious expert wasn't looking for answers; he was looking for a loophole. He asked Jesus to clarify, wondering exactly how far loving his neighbor had to go. "And who is my neighbor?"

The question prompted Jesus to tell a parable in which a man traveling between towns was mugged and left for dead on the side of the road. On two separate occasions, a priest and a Levite (a man who would have served as an aide in the temple) passed him, averting their gazes so as to ignore the helpless man. Finally a Samaritan saw him and took pity on him—a Samaritan, the very picture of the Jewish enemy, a biblical-era bad guy. The Samaritan, contrary to what everyone listening would have believed, bandaged the man's wounds and took him to an inn, even paying the innkeeper for any expenses.

Jesus turned the tables back to the "expert," prompting him to admit that the Samaritan was the most neighborly of the three potential helpers. The religious expert went so far as to say the Samaritan "had mercy on him," and Jesus instructed him, "Go and do likewise" (see Luke 10:25–37).

This story has been told and retold throughout the years, perhaps because it is one of the hardest to digest. It has lost some of its original impact, considering that Samaritans have all but disappeared from the modern political landscape, but it's not difficult to make the application to a modern reader. Jesus instructs this expert in the Law to emulate the *Samaritan*, the very nationality to which the expert would have felt the most personal enmity. The religious people in the story—the priest and the Levite—offer no help to the beaten man, even going so far as to ignore him. The Samaritan, on the other hand, put aside his life and had pity.

I was reminded of my experience on the side of the road, trying desperately to avoid eye contact with the man whose car had broken down. I tried to convince myself that I was right to be cautious in light of my earlier experience, that it was careless to step into the same trap twice. But Jesus' words kept coming back to me: "Go and do likewise." There are no qualifiers to his statement, no "unless it puts you in harm's way," no "unless it costs you something." Over and over. Again and again.

I thought about it another way: Could it be that Jesus is the Good Samaritan in this story and I am the man who has been robbed and left for dead? Perhaps the priest and the Levite represent the religious systems all around me, the religion that I am so often tempted to embrace but only serves to become a loophole for me. Jesus is demonstrating the way in which our love is to far exceed the religious system that always falls short, the system that says, "Sure, I love my neighbor . . . as long as it doesn't cost me."

To think of it this way will surely extend our responsibility as followers of Jesus. Considering all people our neighbors and loving them as Jesus did will almost certainly put us at risk of being taken advantage of, if not physically harmed. Loving this way will cost us our time, if not our money and effort.

Once again I am reminded of the last week of Jesus' life. Knowing his followers would desert him, knowing even that Judas would turn him in to be executed, he loved them. He spent his last meal with them, serving them by washing their feet and teaching them. He prayed for them fervently in the garden only moments before they all ran away. Over and over he loved them, and over and over they didn't understand.

In C. S. Lewis's classic story *The Lion, the Witch, and the Wardrobe*, the children ask about the famous Aslan, fearing their meeting with him after learning that Aslan is a lion, king of beasts. One of the children asks, "Then he isn't safe?" He is told in response, "Who said anything about safe? 'Course he isn't safe. But he's good."[5] Following Jesus is not safe—loving people to the point of personal discomfort, loving your enemies, and spreading the name of Jesus to the ends of the earth cannot be safe. But it is good because *he* is good.

DAY 15: FINDING THE JESUS WAY

1. Who do you most identify with in the story of the Good Samaritan?
2. Stop right now and ask Jesus to give you a heart of compassion toward those in need. Make a list of those whom Jesus brings to your mind.
3. What does it mean for you to "go and do likewise"? Be specific.

Thoughts, Prayers, and Doodles on the Jesus Way

CHAPTER 16

Forgiveness . . . How Many Times?

"I tell you, not seven times, but seventy-seven times."
—Matthew 18:22

Toxic Religion: Forgiveness is often conditional and limited.

The Jesus Way: There is no limit to the forgiveness we receive from Jesus or the forgiveness we are to extend to others.

ave you ever been betrayed or really hurt by someone you trusted? Sure you have. We all have. That's how I felt about Jim. I could tell you the story. I could probably even justify my unforgiving spirit concerning him, but that's not the point. The details no longer matter; they seldom do after a little time has passed.

Jim passed away just the other year. It happened way too soon and he was way too young. He died of an aggressive kind of lung cancer.

Jim and I began our relationship shortly after he had become a follower of Jesus. God had forgiven both of us for so much. We both had a lot to be thankful for and we both were intoxicated by the grace God had extended to us.

But we had a misunderstanding. I felt betrayed. In that betrayal I felt that severing my relationship with him was justifiable. I bet I could convince you it was. It seems that when need be, we can always rationalize our behavior no matter how far off base it might be.

My plan was to write him right out of the plot of my life. I actually did a pretty good job of it. At least until Jim and my sister decided to get married. I was, of course, invited to the wedding, but no one knew if I would actually attend. *I* didn't know if I would attend, even until I walked in the door, moments before the service began.

A Vulnerable Position

Sitting in the back of the church that day, I was in knots. I began to wonder if maybe this is what we mean when we say we are "walking by faith"—I didn't know from one moment to the next what I would do; I was taking one step at a time. As the ceremony progressed, I became aware that God was giving me a mental image to ponder. In it, I was standing at the edge of a cliff in a very vulnerable position. The only thing keeping me from going over was Jim, who was in a position to push me over or pull me back up. God wanted me to intentionally put myself in this position with Jim.

Yet I hadn't spoken to him in years. I had taken control of our relationship, and I was making him pay for his sin (as I perceived it) by withdrawing from his life. From my perspective, I was protecting myself against further hurt and disappointment. Yet God was pushing me to become vulnerable once again, to give up control, to take a big risk. He was urging me to give Jim another chance by letting go of my anger, bitterness, and pain, by forgiving and being forgiven.

I sat conflicted throughout the entire ceremony as my dad gave my sister away, my other sister sang, and my mother sat in her rightful place. I joined the receiving line at the back of the church, still unsure of what I would do when I reached the newlywed couple. I watched as other guests smiled, laughed, and hugged. The line shortened, and the crowd thinned out as the guests made their way to the reception, while I inched closer and closer to Jim and my sister. Taking a deep breath, I took one step toward them. The second and third steps came easier, and by the time I had taken six or seven steps, I was in a confident gait. The few people remaining in the church seemed silent; they were mostly close family and knew about the years of cold indifference I had shown to Jim. As I approached him, I took Jim in my arms and whispered to him, "Take care of my sister."

With those small words, bitterness, resentment, and my refusal to forgive let go of this ugly grip on my heart. My relationship with my new brother-in-law was born again. The old way was gone and the new was coming, with holidays and birthdays and weddings and other special occasions no longer dreaded, but with new life blown into them. The heavy burden of anger was lifted from my very weak shoulders.

Great Reconciler

Jesus came as the Great Reconciler, knowing that forgiveness is a universal need. We fail to forgive, we fail to heal, and brokenness makes a permanent home in our lives. Yet Jesus teaches one of his greatest lessons on forgiveness from the cross, even at his most broken. Hanging by the nails in his hands, his body weight supported by nothing but the nails in his feet, he asks, "Father, forgive them, for they do not know what they are doing" (Luke 23:34).

Forgive them. Forgive the disciples who fell asleep, who went their own way as I was arrested in the garden. Forgive Peter who denied me three times in spite of his insistence that he would never do such a thing. Forgive Judas who betrayed me for a little bit of money. Forgive the conspiring priest, teachers of the law, and the elders. Forgive the mob that blindly shouted, "Crucify him!" at the instruction of the leaders. Forgive the Sanhedrin that used the Law to condemn an innocent man. Forgive the high priest who jumped to his own conclusion of blasphemy. Forgive those who spit on me, blindfolded me, and struck me with their fists. Forgive Pilate who allowed the execution of an innocent man. Forgive those who pounded the nails into my hands and feet. Forgive those who stood at the foot of the cross, insulting me. Forgive David for holding a grudge against Jim.

Keep Forgiving

Peter once came to Jesus, asking, "Lord, how many times shall I forgive my brother when he sins against me? Up to seven times?" Peter knew the Law well, thinking that surely seven times would be enough. Any more would indicate the asker was not truly repentant and, in Peter's view, not deserving of forgiveness. Yet Jesus answered him, "Not seven times, but seventy-seven times" (Matt. 18:21–22). Jesus' implication is that there should be no limit to our forgiveness, and he follows this assertion with a parable that illustrates the fact that the forgiveness we receive is predicated on our willingness to forgive others.

It is impossible to love like Jesus without forgiving like Jesus, as nothing demonstrates love more than forgiveness. Nothing communicated his love for us more than the cross—in the most unforgiving place, Jesus forgives. It is at the cross we are reminded that forgiveness comes at a price someone has to pay. When Jesus paid the ultimate price, not only did he settle our debt, he modeled the way in which we are to respond when we are offended.

There is no room for refusal to forgive in God's kingdom. I love Romans 5:7–8: "For a good man someone might possibly dare to die. But God demonstrates his own love for us in this: While we were *still sinners*, Christ died for us" (emphasis added). His forgiveness reached

us while we were still sinners, and we have no place in the kingdom
when we fail to forgive those who sin against us. He shows us his
love in that he died for us when we weren't worth dying for. Jesus, in
his love, gave up his throne and was born a humble human being. He
took a common name, Jesus, and lived as a servant. He surrendered
his life, redeeming us, no longer holding our sin against us, because
he loves us. It wasn't as if we were fighting our way back, repenting.
We had turned and gone our own ways, but Jesus came fighting for
us, like a parent who never gives up on a wayward child.

No Way Out

How many times? In his question to Jesus, Peter seems to be looking for
a way out. Perhaps he's drawing on an experience in which a friend
asked for forgiveness time and again, and Peter, growing frustrated
and sinking back into his religious ways, aims to find the limit. Jesus'
parable strips away the excess, leaving bare truth for the taking. When
we fail to forgive, we demonstrate the qualities of the unmerciful
servant who, when granted complete forgiveness, refused to grant it
in return (see Matt. 18:23–35).

What's more, Jesus, as he often did, takes forgiveness several
steps further. Not only must we be merciful to those who ask, but we
are to continually ask forgiveness from those we have offended.

Therefore, if you are offering your gift at the altar and
there remember that your brother has something against
you, leave your gift there in front of the altar. First go and

be reconciled to your brother; then come and offer your gift. (Matt. 5:23–24)

Jesus is obviously more concerned about our relationships with others than with our obeying the letter of the law. Relationships have a way of demonstrating our hearts. There's no escaping what they teach us about ourselves. It doesn't matter whether you're right or wrong, Jesus seems to say, but it's up to you to *make* things right by forgiving and asking forgiveness. Granting forgiveness can be difficult, especially when we feel we have been wronged and there is no indication of repentance, but it's the best way and the only way for a follower of Jesus.

Costly Forgiveness

Forgiveness always comes with a cost. When I perceived that Jim had hurt me, I made him pay by withdrawing my relationship and support. Through God's grace, on his wedding day I was able to cancel that debt and forgive Jim. It was up to me to deal with the pain of letting go of my hurt and with the risk of letting him back into my life, and I had to pay the price of reconciliation. But with that debt nearly twenty-five years past, I can hardly remember the cost in light of the joy that came with the redeeming of our friendship.

Forgiveness is not free. On the cross Jesus took all our offenses on himself. He took the payment on himself. In doing so, he reconciled us to himself and granted us a right relationship with him and the Father throughout all eternity.

My Qualifier

I didn't want to include this chapter. It seems too close to home. It reveals too much about me. It exposes my own weakness. At the same time I must. I know that some who read this are stuck where I was stuck. You are not alone. This wasn't the first time for me and it sure won't be the last. Sometimes I am the one offended; other times I am the offender. With Jesus I am always the offender. Jesus is always the forgiver. There is much brokenness in our relationship, yet Jesus came paying an incredible price that we might be reconciled to him. Now we must be willing to die to ourselves and pay a similar debt that others might experience the forgiveness and freedom that come with this kind of love. It is not an easy love. At the end of the day, if one person can experience the forgiveness I have experienced, it is well worth exposing my weaknesses.

DAY 16: FINDING THE JESUS WAY

1. Who is the one person you most need to forgive?
2. What does it look like for you to extend forgiveness to this person?
3. Do whatever it takes to grant this forgiveness in person.

Thoughts, Prayers, and Doodles on the Jesus Way

BOOK THREE

Leaving What Jesus Leaves Behind

Living and loving like Jesus is just the beginning. If Jesus had only lived and loved, his life would have ended with his memory. Because Jesus left behind people who lived like him and loved like him, what began with a life continues as a movement through you and me.

CHAPTER 17

Study Course ... It's Your Life

*Jesus went up on a mountainside and called to him
those he wanted, and they came to him.*

—Mark 3:13

Toxic Religion: The more knowledge I can obtain about God, the more he approves of me.

The Jesus Way: Jesus' life is my study course.

I woke up really tired this morning. Some days I feel as if I'm wearing out. Can you relate? Sometimes when it comes to our mission, I feel the need to do more and more. Doing more and more wears me out. Today as I began my day sitting with Jesus, I prayed for rest concerning our mission. Once again I must ask the question, "What if I'm wrong?" What if we've made our mission way too complicated?

When I first read this passage, I was blown away. (I still am.) I couldn't believe what I was reading. How did I miss it? Maybe I was wrong. Maybe my focus had been on the wrong things. Maybe I needed to do a little repenting.

> Jesus went up on a mountainside and called to him those he wanted, and they came to him. He appointed twelve— designating them apostles—that they might be with him and that he might send them out to preach and to have authority to drive out demons. (Mark 3:13–15)

Did you see it? Not the part about preaching and driving out demons. That's not what grabs me in this passage. Take a second look at it: "He called to him those he wanted, and they came to him." Jesus chose the twelve he wanted so he could teach them to preach and drive out demons. I get that, but look at the preceding part of this verse: "that they might be with him."

It's Not about Curriculum—It's about Doing Life

Jesus' priority wasn't a curriculum. His priority was spending his life in intimate relationships with others. He chose those he wanted to be with. We know them as his disciples, but they were much more. They were his friends, and he chose to spend his life with them. He didn't take them through a study course, an intense Bible study, or a twenty-six-week discipleship program. He simply lived with them. Jesus' life was his study course.

I spent much of my life thinking if I could only find the right curriculum, Bible study, or discipleship course for people to read, their lives would be changed. In many ways all of these can be cop-outs when they are void of relationships. If being a follower of Jesus is about living like Jesus, loving like Jesus, and leaving what Jesus left behind, we have to ask the question, "How did Jesus leave behind people who lived like him and loved like him?" The answer is right here—he chose those he wanted to live life with, he loved them, and he told them to go and do the same. All this was done in the context of real life.

How do we leave what Jesus left behind? We do the things Jesus did—we surround ourselves with the people he wants us to be with and we do life together in the context of following Jesus and his ways. Don't be surprised that he might choose these people for us. Notice when Jesus chose his twelve, he didn't find them on the temple steps. In the same way, don't be surprised by those he may choose for you to do life with. I promise you it won't be all your friends from church. Jesus chose twelve men that they might know him—disconnected, broken, foolish, brash, annoying, and smelly men. In the context of doing real life together, we show them the Jesus way through our successes and failures, high times and low times, in good times and bad.

In many ways, what I am coming to understand about the Jesus way is much more challenging than my old religious ways. No longer is it enough to line up three guys to do a Bible study at 6:00 a.m. on Monday; now I must open up my life and my time to them. Like the disciples with Jesus, they have total access to me. My time with them may—and often does—still involve curriculum, Bible studies, and study courses, but they are done in the context of real life together. I'm not against gaining more knowledge about Jesus and his ways. Often, learning about his ways begins there, but frankly some of the meanest people I know have a lot of Bible knowledge. We need to understand that curriculum, Bible studies, and study courses are no longer an end, but rather a means to an end.

Just as Jesus *was* the study course for the twelve he chose, Jesus' life lived through us *is* the study course for those we choose to do life with. He lives in us, changing us and changing others through us. That's why it is so important that we live and love like Jesus.

You Don't Know Me

For many of us this seems too simple, especially if our lives are complicated by religion. When we focus on our religion, things become all about *us*. But when we focus on living like Jesus and loving like Jesus, we inevitably leave what Jesus left behind: more people who live and love like Jesus.

You may object to the idea that God could use your life to impact others. You may wonder how you can invest your life in someone else when your life is so messy. Or perhaps you are far too busy and lack the relationship skills to give your life to others. In all of these cases, there is good news for you. Jesus alone holds the power to change lives. He never expected us, with our messed-up lives and neurotic social tendencies, to generate a message of hope and deliverance from our own power. He expects us to, like John the Baptist, point the way to himself. The amazing thing is when we take this journey our lives are changed in the process.

For much of my life I viewed my relationship with Jesus through the lens of activity. I felt I had to always be doing something and accomplishing something in order to meet his approval. However, in reading Mark's description of Jesus' life with the disciples, I am coming to recognize there are many things keeping me from these kinds of significant relationships. When I made a commitment to follow Jesus and understood that following him meant living like him, I began to pay close attention to how he lived his life so that I might live and love like him.

It's about Relationships

The Jesus way is simple. However, just because it's simple doesn't mean it is void of purpose. Jesus was filled with purpose, but he also clearly demonstrated that his purpose was all about relationships. Jesus came to Earth, redeeming us in order that we might live and love like him, and there is no bigger purpose in the universe.

Take a moment to read the Great Commandment in Matthew 22:36–40: "'Love the Lord your God. . . . Love your neighbor as yourself.'" When one religious expert asked Jesus what was the most important commandment, Jesus flipped the question by driving home the fact that the entire Law could be boiled down to one thing:

relationships. Nothing was more important to him than our love for God and people.

The Jesus way places our efforts on relationships, yet we have made it about ritual. We treat people as a means to an end, instead of seeing that they *are* the end and that God created us for each other. Jesus invites us into a relationship with himself, and we in turn extend the same invitation to others. It should be something like, "Come follow me as I follow him" (see I Cor. 11:1).

When I focus on tasks at the expense of people, I lose my way. When I trust a system more than the power Jesus has instilled in me, I disobey his command to love God and love others. I recognized that if I was going to live like Jesus, love like Jesus, and ultimately leave what Jesus left behind, I was going to have to let him do a new work in and through me. I would have to learn to relate to people rather than tasks, to spend time developing life with people rather than in accomplishments. This was going to involve a reordering of my life. It would require rethinking and repenting.

Full Exposure and Disclosure

Overwhelmed by the simplicity of this verse, I could not deny the priority of investing my life in a few others. Jesus called together twelve ordinary men and committed himself to them constantly for three years. They were allowed access to every dimension of his life, sharing his thoughts, explaining his kingdom, modeling the way of God, encouraging them, challenging them. They learned how to love by being loved by him. They learned how to encourage as they received his encouragement. They learned to forgive when he extended forgiveness to them. They learned how to overcome their own prejudice as they crossed the borders of Samaria with him leading the way.

When we talk about "doing life" together, we usually have in mind spending a few hours a week with a few people in a small group. When Jesus "does life" with someone, it's full-on exposure to every part of his heart and mind, all day every day.

Living the Jesus way means opening up our lives to a few that we choose to do life with. As you journey through the ups and downs of life, you learn together. You struggle together. You succeed together. They will see your sin, and you will confess together. You will hurt, and they will understand your pain. They must be invited into the well-ordered rooms of your life as well as into the messy rooms. They will follow you as you follow Jesus. It is out of this context of real life together that you will discover Jesus and his ways and, I hope, choose to embrace him and his ways.

Making Room

Over the years Tami and I have expanded the outdoor living area of our home. When we first moved into our house, the rear of our house consisted of a second level 10 x 12 deck that you could access only through a set of sliding doors off the kitchen. Today it consists of a sprawling (maybe an overstatement, but it's sprawling to us) deck that encompasses the entire length of our house. Under it is a concrete patio that covers the same space. Trees, plants, and a small pond complete with a waterfall have transformed this space into a place where we do life with our friends and family. As Jesus has transformed our lives, we have made room in our schedule for those special people. It is here they are exposed to every aspect of our life. Almost every week someone will call and say something like, "We are bringing supper over and want to do a little life." We have made it a point to make these kinds of moments and relationships an intentional part of our lives and, at the same time, spontaneous part of our life. We want to be available for them and they for us. It is here that the curriculum of our lives is regularly laid out before them.

This life requires a major detoxing from busyness and a reordering of our need to have everything perfect and in place. This kind of life forces us to constantly create more and more margin in our lives. It is here that we are seeing lives changed. It is here that we are seeing our lives change.

DAY 17: FINDING THE JESUS WAY

1. What can you learn from Jesus about doing life with others?
2. How can curriculum help you or hinder you from discovering the Jesus way?
3. Who are the people God is putting in your life and calling you to do life with?

Thoughts, Prayers, and Doodles on the Jesus Way

CHAPTER 18

Disciples . . . You've Got to Be One to Make One

"Therefore go and make disciples of all nations."
—Matthew 28:19

> **Toxic Religion:** We build large organizations that cater to the needs of religious consumers.
>
> **The Jesus Way:** Our mission is to make disciples.

We live in amazing times. There is much conversation about our changing world. We are experiencing major cultural shifts. The old is going and the new is emerging. Our modern world has been replaced with a postmodern world. The dust is settling, and Jesus' words are clearer than ever: "As the Father has sent me, I am sending you" (John 20:21). The harvest is indeed white unto harvest.

Our heavenly Father is a missionary God. Jesus is a missionary Savior. We are a missionary people empowered with his Spirit, sent into this amazing world to live, love, and leave what Jesus left behind. At the same time, we often feel unprepared. Even our churches leave us unprepared. Being a missional people requires repenting. Being missional involves rediscovering the simplicity of Jesus and his ways. Yes, that's right, complexity is out and simplicity is in. Let's take a look.

Going Retro

God is calling us to reimagine our core mission: the Great Commission. "'Therefore go and make disciples of all nations, baptizing them in the name of the Father and of the Son and of the Holy Spirit, and teaching them to obey everything I have commanded you. And surely I am with you always, to the very end of the age'" (Matt. 28:19–20).

God is calling us back to the Great Commission. This may surprise you because you may be unaware we ever left it. Maybe you haven't personally, but many have. Going retro means remembering we all have the same mission—to "go and make disciples." When we live life with Jesus and love people as he did, we can't help but be drawn into his heart for the lost and the world. We can't help but be about this disciple-making life. As the church this is our primary mission. There is no other mission. Many have made the church about so much more. Making disciples is "the more."

What is a disciple? It's exactly what we have been talking about all along. A disciple is a follower of Jesus who lives like him, loves like him, and leaves what he left behind, which are others who live like him and love like him. As a missional people, there is no other way. This is who we are. This is what we do. The kingdom of heaven is at hand and Jesus invites us into it. As we live his way, his kingdom comes. This is the mission we must return to—this is the mission of our lives.

While there are many worthy causes that capture our attention as a church and a people of God, we must realize that our significance is not in how many religious or humanitarian activities we involve ourselves. When we focus on making disciples, all this stuff happens. The bottom line is how are we doing when it comes to our disciple-making mission? How are we doing in making "little Christs" as the early church called believers? How are we doing in leaving little Christs behind us?

This is not to say we all look the same or approach our mission in the same exact way. While our core mission is the same, our vision for accomplishing this mission is often very different. God has created, gifted, and wired all of us in unique ways. He has placed us in very different contexts that require a missional understanding in order to fulfill our mission. God has given all of us the ability to imagine, dream, and envision his kingdom coming on Earth as it is in heaven. We all have our unique stories. We all have things we feel most passionate about. God uses our uniqueness to shape within our hearts a vision for how we fulfill our disciple-making mission. For me, I write (my gift), lead an organization for church planters (my passion), and lead others in going around the world to install water systems, train international pastors, and help further the kingdom (my method and life). Yet my—no, our—mission is the same.

God has given us all the capacity for a redemptive imagination that allows us to envision what our churches, families, and lives could be like if God had his way in this disciple-making mission. This is the work of his Spirit within us. He promises us that he is able to do abundantly above all that we ask or think (see Eph. 3:18–21). We call this vision. However, this vision is always connected back to our mission: making disciples. This is where we must begin.

Rediscovering Jesus

Making disciples begins with rediscovering Jesus. I recently spoke with a young pastor who had visited one of the healthiest church plants in our city. They are just a few months old but already have nearly three hundred people in their weekend services. Its amazing growth seems unlimited. My friend began by describing all the things the young church was doing right. As he listed them, it seemed he was describing a product we consume. In this case the product was a weekend worship service. He talked about things like parking, contemporary music, quality child care, and applicable teaching about real-life issues. The list went on and on. When he paused, I asked him if Jesus was in the church. He stopped and seemed to struggle with my question. He wanted me to clarify what I meant. I reframed my question by asking if, in the midst of all the church did, Jesus was the central focus. Did everything point to him? He stopped as if he were taking a mental inventory and finally concluded, "Not really." His heart was broken by this new revelation.

This young church was obviously building a great organization, but Jesus had somehow slipped out the back door. I'm sensitive to this tendency to nudge Jesus out the back door because of my own experience. I didn't ask him this question to be negative or to call what this church is doing into question. I asked him because there have been times in my own life and ministry when I have been so eager and impressed with my own religion that I have left Jesus out of it. Let's face it, we all feel this tension when it comes to being a missional people. We want to be culturally relevant and biblically faithful. Sometimes we opt for cool, cute, or relevant over Christ centered. When we attempt to connect with a culture far from God, we must be careful not to throw the baby out with the bathwater (in this case, the baby is Jesus). Remember, Jesus is relevant!

Over the past few decades, there has been a tendency to put our ecclesiology before our Christology or, in simpler terms, to put our churches or religious expressions before Jesus. We allow culture to shape our churches and then churches to shape our Jesus. Fortunately, this trend is changing. Many of us are rediscovering the centrality and the simplicity of Jesus and his ways in our lives and churches. This is a good thing. This is a must.

Living a missional life requires continually shifting back to Jesus. Recently I experienced this in my life when I realized I was caught up in my own ministry, my own quiet time, and my own belief system.

Put it on a list, and I would have checked off all the stuff we call essential to our faith. At the same time, I had slowly pushed Jesus out of my life and ministry. I had lost my way and didn't even know it. Since that time I have been rediscovering Jesus and his ways.

When we focus our ministry on *our* religion, we build forms, structures, and rules that leave little or no room for Jesus. The difference can be subtle. Both ecclesiology (our understanding of church) and Christology (our understanding of Jesus) are required in missional living, but we must begin with a healthy Christology if we are going to live missional lives. Missional living flows first from a relationship with Jesus, and then flows naturally into relationships with others. Our structures—our churches and curriculum—should support, not take over. The focus should never be our structures; it is always Jesus. When we begin with Jesus, our churches will take on a kind of Christlikeness.

Be a Disciple

When we take the mission of making disciples seriously, it's a sobering reality that I'm going to reproduce what I am. This is why it is so important we begin with a healthy Christology. This is why it is so important we have a clear understanding of what it means to be a follower of Jesus, along with a clear understanding that our ministry overflows from this understanding and relationship. It is about me choosing to walk with Jesus daily, knowing that as I remain in him he bears much fruit through my life (see John 15:5).

As I said earlier, leaving what Jesus left behind is not about a curriculum, Bible study, or study course—it's about following Jesus. God has chosen to show us his way through his Word, which is why I have been reading and rereading the Gospels. He is the Truth that sets us free from all religion. Being a disciple is a prerequisite to being able to make disciples. We are always going to reproduce what we are.

Make Disciples

Following Jesus in today's missional environment can be intimidating and sometimes overwhelming. The field on which we play is often hostile and unfriendly toward the church and the gospel. Many people no longer have a Christian memory. Most of us are equipped to minister in a world that favors religion, but our Western world is increasingly disconnected from a biblical worldview. Our best success as the organized church has been generated by focusing on reaching, caring, and engaging those who have a Christian memory. The future calls for a massive gear shift—not to reject this segment but to include more aggressively those who are far from God. This means ministry must look different.

By refocusing on disciple making, we can all participate, no matter what playing field we find ourselves on. I recently spoke to a number of different groups across the United States. I began on the East Coast in a very traditional Bible Belt community where many of the churches' greatest concerns were survival. From there

I went to the Midwest where I spoke to college students who face the challenge of reaching their peers who are far from God. I wrapped up my trip in the Northwest by speaking to another group of followers who are trying to reach one of the most unreached areas of our country.

While their challenges are different, the solution is the same: Begin by making disciples. We can all start there. When it comes to making disciples, we are not limited by resources—it takes only one person who is committed to live, love, and leave like Jesus to have an immeasurable impact on our world. When we as disciples take his word with us in the power and the understanding of his Spirit, we need nothing else. This is good news for the church no matter what we face.

As I traveled across the country, in many ways it felt as if I was preaching the gospel to the church and people were hearing it for the very first time. The truth is that many of us are hearing it for the first time in a long time. Followers of Jesus all over the country are ready to rediscover Jesus. They are embracing the message and are moving toward missional lives with excitement and new energy. People everywhere want to know how to leave their religion behind and start living missionally. The church as we know it is prime for this kind of conversion.

We are all on a level playing field. Jesus' method for making disciples hasn't changed. Regardless of our context, we can all begin right now, right here.

DAY 18: FINDING THE JESUS WAY

1. When it comes to the Great Commission, have you lost your way? How?
2. Why is it so important that disciple making begins and ends with Jesus?
3. Why does it take being a disciple to make a disciple?
4. What does rediscovering the Great Commission look like for you? Be specific.

Thoughts, Prayers, and Doodles on the Jesus Way

_____

_____

_____

_____

_____

_____

_____

_____

_____

_____

_____

_____

CHAPTER 19

Go . . . Stop Praying and Start Going

*"And when you pray, do not keep on babbling like pagans,
for they think they will be heard because of their many
words. Do not be like them, for your Father knows
what you need before you ask him."*
—Matthew 6:7–8

Toxic Religion: Going is a profession that is
reserved for the religious elite.

The Jesus Way: Jesus qualifies the unqualified.

As I write this, I am flying toward the Middle East with the purpose of training pastors in the Jesus way. This is one of several trips I've taken this year, and in a few months I'll be headed to another part of the Middle East, this time smuggling Bibles to those who are seeking to discover Jesus and his ways. It is simply amazing what God is up to in the Middle East. People by the ten thousands who are far from God are finding him. But it doesn't end there—God is at work everywhere. These are good times to be engaged in God's mission.

We Must Go

As I take these trips, I run into more and more resistance from people in the West. They tell me I am at risk, and that it's much safer to stay home. They tell me we should all stay home until the unrest settles down, and usually they heed their own advice. Yet I am compelled to go. As I go, I am discovering that many in the Middle East are already finding the Jesus way. God is at work. They are my brothers and sisters, and many of them are suffering at the hands of persecution. If nothing else, by going we bring encouragement to them and accountability to those persecuting them. And the more I visit these countries, the more I become aware of our kinship in Jesus. On one occasion in Mark's account of Jesus' life, Jesus' mother and brothers came to seek him out. The Scriptures indicate they were concerned about Jesus' strange behavior, and the crowd alerts Jesus to the fact that his family is looking for him. I can see Jesus now, looking at those around him, waving his arms, saying, "Here are my mother and my brothers! Whoever does God's will is my brother and sister and mother" (Mark 3:34–35).

That's what is happening to me as I travel. More and more, relational barriers are being broken down, and I am realizing that our brothers, sisters, and mothers are crying out for help. We must respond. It is our responsibility. It is the way of love. If they suffer, we suffer. If they are in need, we are in need. If they are blessed, we are blessed. We are one in Christ, and that's why we must go. Going is not optional. It is the Jesus way. And in today's world many of us, if not most of us, are without excuse.

Stop Praying

Sometimes you have to stop in order to start, and I think this is especially true when it comes to our mission of going. When it comes to going and making disciples, some people only pray; they never get to the going part. Almost every week someone says to me, "I'm praying about going." Others say to me, "I really want to go; I am praying about it." We often toss around going as if it's some kind of religious preference or option. That's why I consistently tell people to stop praying and start going. Why do we need to pray about something that Jesus is so clear about? The Great Commission is for all of us. Jesus didn't instruct us to pray about following him, but he demonstrated that following him is a natural part of our lives that will always lead us to the very ends of the earth (see Acts 1:8).

It's a Command, Not a Suggestion

This command to go is for all of us who are committed to living the Jesus way. It may be a natural part of the flesh to wrestle with the Spirit, but to not have any desire at all, to have no compassion for those without Jesus, indicates our need to repent. In my view, we have two options: Go or repent and then go. When we see a need that Jesus would meet, we see an invitation to go. When we see Jesus at work, we see our invitation to join him.

I mentioned earlier that many people were becoming followers of Jesus in a particular country in the Middle East. The result is a need for house-church pastors to be trained and Bibles to be smuggled—this was my invitation. I don't need to pray about whether or not I should go, I simply need to go.

Religion Can Keep Us from Going

There are many reasons we don't go. Religion tells us we are not good enough to go. Jesus says, "It is my righteousness that counts!" Religion tells us we have to be qualified. Jesus tells us we will be his witnesses once we have received the Holy Spirit (Acts 1:8). Religion tells us it will cost too much, that it will take both our time and our money. Jesus tells us that where our treasure is our heart will be also (Matt. 6:21). Religion tells us that some are called to make disciples and others are called to different things. Jesus tells us all to go and make disciples and promises us that he will be with us until the very end (Matt. 28:19–20). Religion often divides us based on our different cultures and preferences. Jesus comes to unite us and make us one people.

Going Is the Jesus Way

If Jesus is living in you and moving you to love, you are a missionary. Going is what we are called, qualified, and commissioned to do. As long as there are people far from God, in need of his love, we must go. In an overly religious culture, going is reserved for those who are set apart by traditions, and as a result only a few are "qualified." However, when you look at what Jesus said and the way he lived, it becomes clear that those who hear his voice and respond have received their qualification in full.

Before you panic, remember that *go* doesn't have to mean go to Africa or go somewhere dangerous. It might simply mean go to your front porch or go into your community. I used to think the only way I could fulfill the Great Commission was to jump on a jet for twenty hours and land in a place with no telephones. In many ways, today the world comes to us. *Going* also means opening our arms and our churches and receiving the people who want to come in. It might mean reentering your community. We have isolated ourselves, leaving our cities, communities, and neighborhoods for peace and solitude, and in the process we've abandoned our neighbors.

I often run into people who ask me to pray for them. They tell me, "There are no Christians where I work. I want a job where there is more of a Christian environment." But I'm not praying for them, at least not in the way they ask. I *am* praying, however, they will come to understand that following Jesus and his ways is about going *into* the world, not isolating oneself *from* the world.

It's amazing how quickly we find ourselves trapped in our holy huddles. This has always been true. It didn't take the infant church long to do likewise—it wasn't until a great persecution against the church in Jerusalem broke out that it was scattered throughout Judea and Samaria (see Acts 8). Sometimes Jesus has to shake up our lives in order to get us going.

Going is an attitude. It's about having the mind of Christ. It is a commitment to seeking out those who are far from God and in need of him—no matter whether they're in the Middle East or the house next door. It is the attitude of Jesus who came to seek and save those who were lost. Going inevitably means we allow Jesus to push us way out of our comfort zones, challenging us to go when we would rather stay safe and comfortable.

Going Begins Right Where You Are

Recently I was challenged to go by staying. My son had just returned from a fifteen-month deployment to Afghanistan. On my way to the gym one afternoon, Tami informed me that my son was coming home for the weekend. I was so excited. At least until she went on to tell me that he was bringing some of his Army buddies home with him. Have you been around any Army buddies who have just spent fifteen months in a war? I immediately reacted. I thought of my daughter. I thought of my home. I thought of a lot of things and told her I didn't want a bunch of single Army guys ready to raise heck coming with him.

Tami did what she does so well; she gave me a little space. When I got on the treadmill at the gym, God began to speak really loud. By the time I got back in the car to head home, I was worn out and ready to repent. She was right and I was wrong. I told her that our home would always be open to these young soldiers who had laid it on the line for our freedom. I went on to tell her to tell our son to bring the whole stinking Army with him. I meant it! Over the past year I don't think he's brought the whole stinking Army, just a big part of it. Our home has become a refuge for my son and his fellow soldiers. These soldiers come from all kinds of backgrounds. Many of them have little or no Christian background. They come as they are and we receive them as they are. Our goal is to live, love, and leave. They have become our family.

My favorite time with them is when we prepare a big meal together. They love to eat and drink (not milk). When we share a meal together, I gather them in a big circle, we join hands, and I pray thanking God for them and praying for their upcoming deployment. It's one of the ways I go without leaving my house. Soon they will redeploy to one of the most dangerous places in the world. I am so glad that Tami and I have opened our home and our hearts to these guys. We will spend much time over the next year praying for them, sending them packages, and posting notes to them on Facebook. When they return, we will once again open our home. They are our mission and we accept it with honor. They are our friends.

There is something radical about the nature of God's call in our lives. Part of it has to do with the sheer simplicity of going.

Following Jesus is not a profession—following Jesus is a way of life. Like the disciples, we get the training we need as we go. Following Jesus means that we are to follow him. It's that easy.

Stop praying and start going.

DAY 19: FINDING THE JESUS WAY

1. What does it mean for you to stop praying and start going?
2. What are some ways you can be involved right where you live?
3. What about the rest of the world? Where is Jesus inviting you to go?

Thoughts, Prayers, and Doodles on the Jesus Way

_____

_____

_____

_____

_____

_____

_____

_____

_____

Purpose . . . Just Do It!

"But seek first his kingdom and his righteousness, and all these things will be given to you as well."
—Matthew 6:33

Toxic Religion: We are defined by the positions we hold.

The Jesus Way: Jesus is our purpose.

I have a restless spirit. Can you relate? For me the grass always looks greener on the other side of the fence, and I have my hands in many different things. A few years ago I took a personality profile that came back describing me as someone who likes one exciting challenge after the other. Precisely! I get bored easily, and I constantly feel compelled to do something, often going and going until I run out of steam. Once I recuperate, I'm off again. I'm either on top of the world or way down in the valley. As I said earlier, I've always been this way—a normal, healthy, dysfunctional, ADHD (I think my ADHD has ADD) kind of guy.

Spiritual Breakthrough

Lately I've hit a new gear. I've had a spiritual breakthrough and have been experiencing more synergy in my life than ever before. Things are really coming together. There is a kind of laser focus in my life like never before. I used to think that pursuing the right post or position would lead to this kind of synergy. I'm discovering that position or place has very little to do with it. The truth is when you accept Jesus' invitation to follow him, he becomes your purpose. And when your life is no longer about you and Jesus is your purpose, there is no limit to what God can do in you and through you. Your life takes on a new kind of significance, and you are set up to have an amazing impact.

Maybe you can relate. We all want our lives to count. We have this ache in our soul that keeps us asking, "Why am I here?" Pause and count how many times you have asked or been asked, "How can I know God's will for my life?"

It's Not about the Place

Most of us live as if we think the answer has something to do with the place we work or the position we fill. I can certainly relate to that.

Several years ago I worked in an organization that was experiencing unprecedented change. Since I wasn't responsible for the change, I wanted out. I felt that if I could get out and find the right place to serve, I would be happy. During this time, I landed on the short list of candidates for a key ministry position in another part of the country. I was overjoyed, convinced that the antidote to my discontentment was a new position in a new town and with a good raise. This organization flew me to its headquarters for an interview. I was familiar with the organization and regarded highly many of the people who served in it. Furthermore, the city where it was located was one of my favorite places in the country. On the flight to the interview, I was confident I would fit in perfectly and do a great job there.

By the time the interview ended and I was boarding my return flight, I knew something was wrong. If offered the position, I wasn't going to be able to take it. During the interview process, I realized I was carrying around tons of unfinished emotional business related to my current position. I knew that no move would fix it. I realized that if I moved, I would take me with me, so I decided I better start by working on me. On my flight home I began making a list of the many things I needed to address about myself, and for the next few years I accepted this list as my assignment from God. I guess you could have called it the "Me Project." By the time I got off the plane, I was totally energized. I was on a mission, and my journal had a list of eleven things I knew only I could address.

Working on *me* changed my life. I no longer found myself worried about the problems and challenges of my current role or the people around me. I even found myself hitting a new gear, and some of the things I didn't like about my job ceased to bother me. About the time I was able to check off many of the things in my journal, I was approached for a new opportunity within my organization. It came out of the blue, and it seemed to really fit who I was. The funny thing was it also gave me the chance to focus on changing the things I didn't like about the organization. For the next couple of years I threw myself at this new position, learning that freedom, peace, and sense of purpose had more to do with my heart than my position.

Jesus Is Our Purpose

What I discovered as I worked on *me* was that the most important thing in my life—my highest purpose—is my relationship with Jesus. There is a reason that Jesus tells us to "seek first his kingdom and his righteousness." When he is first, everything else has a way of finding its place and working out. When he is first and when I understand that he is the purpose for my life, I can accomplish his purpose no matter where I am, no matter my position, no matter my status.

This was my spiritual breakthrough. That's why I do everything I do. I am discovering more and more every day that my purpose has less to do with my position and more to do with Jesus. The challenge is that when we pursue position, place, status, and role over Jesus, he is no longer our purpose. We put the proverbial cart before the horse. Jesus is not a means to an end—Jesus is the beginning and the end. As he put it, "I am the Alpha and the Omega, the First and the Last, the Beginning and the End" (Rev. 22:13). When my life becomes more about position and place, it has a way of pushing him, ever so gently, outside my life.

When Jesus is my purpose, position doesn't matter. What does matter is my understanding of what my mission looks like. If you asked me what my mission is, I would tell you it is rediscovering the simplicity of Jesus and his ways. But it doesn't end there. As I rediscover Jesus, it becomes my responsibility to help others discover and rediscover him. It must never be about me.

With Jesus as my purpose and my mission of rediscovering and helping others rediscover him fixed firmly in my heart and mind, I can accomplish this calling in any position, circumstance, or place. God's will transcends space, place, and time. Rick Warren sums it up beautifully in *The Purpose Driven Life*:

> The purpose of your life is far greater than your own personal fulfillment, your peace of mind, or even your happiness. It's far greater than your family, your career, or even your wildest dreams and ambitions. If you want to know why you were placed on this planet, you must begin with God. You were born by his purpose and for his purpose.[6]

Since becoming purpose-driven (Rick would be proud of me), I have realized that my circumstances have very little to do with what God wants to accomplish in and through me. Wherever I find myself, I can be in the will of God.

I went on to stay in the role I described above for two of the best years of my ministry, and these years included my best service to the organization. Eventually there came a time I did feel it was time to leave. Then I accepted a position in a new church in the community where I lived, serving a group of pastors—anywhere from ten to twenty years younger than I. Some of my closest friends didn't understand this move—a move requiring me to give up my position, corner office, expense account, and nice salary. I'm not sure I understood it either, especially when my new boss walked me around our start-up church and showed me a packed closet I could potentially clean out to use for my new office. The funny thing is, as I write this, I don't have an office. I gave it up about a month ago to make room for two new employees in our growing church. Now before you think too much of me, I am moving into a new office in our new building that will be opening soon, and it is really going to be fancy.

Here is what I am learning: As a pastor in my local church, I can accomplish this purpose. As a leader of a church-planting organization, I can accomplish this purpose. As a writer, I can accomplish this purpose. As a husband, parent, and friend, I can accomplish this purpose. In good times or bad, I can accomplish this purpose. In good health or bad, I can accomplish this purpose. On the other hand, I can have the right title, the most sought-after position, the nicest corner office, the largest salary, and the greatest perks and still miss out on God's purpose for my life.

When we seek Jesus and his ways first, we are promised everything we need. Many of us have spent way too much time trying to fix our situations or circumstances. Religion almost always focuses on what we have or don't have, but Jesus invites us into a whole new way of life that is lived from the inside out. When we live out Jesus as our purpose, then and only then can we leave what Jesus left behind.

DAY 20: FINDING THE JESUS WAY

1. Describe a time in your life when you felt that the answer to finding the Jesus way was a new position or place.
2. What does making Jesus your purpose look like in your life?

Thoughts, Prayers, and Doodles on the Jesus Way

_____

_____

_____

_____

_____

_____

_____

_____

_____

_____

_____

_____

_____

_____

_____

_____

_____

CHAPTER 21

Hospitality . . . Not Another Potluck

*"The kingdom of heaven is like a king who prepared
a wedding banquet."*

—Matthew 22:2

> **Toxic Religion:** Religion is reserved for those
> most like me.
>
> **The Jesus Way:** Following Jesus involves
> extending hospitality to those who are in
> greatest need.

We had a potluck. We don't have them very often, but occasionally we go retro. Even though our spiritual community (church) is made up of many young people with no prior Christian memory, they love this timeless tradition taken right out of the pages of the Deep South's spiritual almanac. That's when I couldn't help but ask the question, "What would Jesus' potlucks have looked like?" Are we talking Dixie cups and sweet tea, or would they have been radically different? Would we as his followers be at home with him, or would his party skills push us to the edge of our comfort zones?

Why not take a look into the party life of Jesus?

The Good Stuff

The scene is Cana in Galilee. The occasion is a wedding, and Jesus was a guest, not the host. The wine runs out. It's a potentially embarrassing moment, equivalent to placing an empty fried chicken bucket into the hands of the visiting evangelist at a Baptist church meeting. It was also a potentially disastrous moment, as a new bride's wedding party was about to be ruined. Jesus' mother springs into action, giving him a little motherly encouragement to save the day. He protests. She insists. He responds. The servants fill the jars with water that are normally reserved for ceremonial washing, and Jesus performs his first miracle, turning the water into wine. The host drinks, observing that this wine is not the cheap stuff that only fraternity boys and drunks enjoy. The host then commends the bridegroom, saying, "Normally the best wine is served first, and the cheap wine is served only after the guests were too drunk to tell the difference, but you have saved the best for last" (John 2:10, author paraphrase).

There are all kinds of spiritual significance in this story: Jesus is at a wedding; the church is Jesus' bride. Jesus has saved the best for last; he himself is the good stuff, the best wine. Jesus has water poured into jars reserved for ceremonial cleansing, and this water is turned into wine. Jesus washes away our sins, doing away with any need for the old religious system, and replaces our old systems with a new Spirit—the Spirit that fills our lives and overshadows the old wine. The old wine (religion) leaves us thirsty and unsatisfied; Jesus' new wine fills us up, leaving us completely satisfied. This party is a celebration—out with the old and in with the new. The symbol is complete, and no longer do we need to be cleaned on the outside; the wine fills us, making us clean from the inside out. What the old wine (religion) couldn't do, the new could. The host (God) has indeed saved the best for last.

On another occasion Jesus stumbled upon a tax collector named Matthew. Tax collectors were the party animals of Jesus' day, known for fancy dinners and good wine. Jesus invited Matthew to follow him, yet to Matthew's surprise, they ended up right back at Matthew's house, where other tax collectors and sinners joined them. What began with a simple "Follow me" turned into an all-out party, greatly offending the religious rulers. They wanted to know, "Why does your teacher eat with tax collectors and 'sinners'?" The disciples had no answer, but Jesus always did: "It is not the healthy who need a doctor, but the sick. I have not come to call the righteous, but sinners" (Mark 2:17). It is here that Jesus began to develop his reputation, according to the religious rulers, as a "drunkard" and a "friend of sinners," which, along with other things, eventually leads to his crucifixion.

The Eccentric Host

But there's more. In Luke 14 Jesus told the parable of the Great Banquet. What is Jesus up to? He ripped into the religious leaders for the way they conduct their parties, inviting just their friends. They invited Jesus only to attempt to trap him and make him some kind of religious sideshow. Yet Jesus turned this encounter on its head. He always does. He drove his point home. When invited, be humble. When you throw a party, invite the poor and crippled. Blessing comes in accepting Jesus' offer to join him. Sadly, the religious leaders were too busy, too focused on themselves to come to the Great Banquet.

In this parable the guest list is complete and the food has been prepared. For one reason or another, none of the preferred guests show up. This is a massive insult to the host, who has gone to great expense for the banquet, and the food is about to spoil. Frederick Buechner helps us focus on what is really happening in his book, *Telling the Truth: The Gospel as Tragedy, Comedy, and Fairy Tale.*

> God is the eccentric host who, when the country-club
> crowd all turn out to have other things more important to
> do than come live it up with him, goes out into the skid
> rows and soup kitchens and charity wards and brings home
> a freak show. The man with no legs who sells shoelaces
> at the corner. The old woman in the moth-eaten fur coat
> who makes her daily rounds of the garbage cans. The old
> wino with his pint in a brown paper bag. The pusher, the
> whore, the village idiot who stands at the blinker light

waving his hand as the cars go by. They are seated at the
damask-laid table in the great hall. The candles are all lit
and the champagne glasses filled. At a sign from the host,
the musicians in their gallery strike up "Amazing Grace."
If you have to explain it, don't bother.[7]

Upon hearing this parable, the tax collectors and sinners gathered around him, entranced by his stories. They had never heard anyone speak with such authority and power, not even the Pharisees and
the teachers of the law. They were muttering, saying, "This man
welcomes sinners and eats with them" (Luke 15:2). This was good
news!

In rapid-fire succession, Jesus told story after story driving his
point home. He began with the story of the Good Shepherd who
left ninety-nine of his sheep so he might find the one that has lost its
way. The Good Shepherd returned, his mission successful, carrying
the once-lost sheep safely on his shoulders. He called his neighbors
together and a party broke out, and Jesus made a point: "I tell you
that in the same way there is more rejoicing in heaven over one sinner who repents than over ninety-nine righteous persons who do not
need to repent" (Luke 15:7).

On another occasion a woman lost something valuable to her—a
silver coin. She spent her night sweeping the house, searching everywhere until she found it. In finding it, there was great rejoicing. She
called her friends, and a party ensued.

There's one final story, a big one. A man had two sons, and
the younger son requested his inheritance and headed off to live the

party life. Before long, he was out of money and out of luck. He came to his senses and began the long journey home, having prepared a speech, hoping for forgiveness.

The father continued to wait, having never stopped waiting from the moment his younger son left home. Finally from his vantage point high in the house, he saw the son returning. No speech was needed, only a celebration—a robe, a ring, some beef, a band, and the best wine—nothing was too good for his son who was lost but now was found (see Luke 15:11–32).

Standing on the Wrong Side

In all of these stories, parables, and examples from Jesus' own life, we find Jesus celebrating those who seem to be on the wrong side. Imagine witnessing all this as a Pharisee—you've worked your whole life to obey every Jewish law down to the letter, yet the man who claims to be the Messiah spends most of his time with sinners? He tells stories about people being celebrated who disobey their parents and God. Jesus is the host who sets the table and fills the glasses so the fringe members of society can partake. Jesus is found leading the choir of ten thousand angels who sing to celebrate finding one lost sheep.

Jesus reconciles us to God and to each other. He is the ultimate party host, granting his hospitality to all people as our primary means of reconciliation. He invites us to sit at the best table, to drink the best wine, and to eat the best meat—to enjoy his salvation.

Jesus grew up in a Jewish culture rife with celebration, where feasts were regularly held in remembrance of God's faithfulness. Just as he invited us into his celebration while we were the dirtiest and foulest of sinners, so, too, must we extend the invitation even to the least among us.

Living like Jesus, loving like Jesus, and leaving what Jesus left behind push us away from the comfort of our suburban fortresses, tea groups, ladies' conferences, men's retreats, and potlucks and into the highways and byways of life where those who live on the edges and fringes reside. Leaving what Jesus left behind pushes us out of comfort and into the role of the eccentric host.

Extending this hospitality opens doors to a world we may hesitate to enter. Those who dare to open the door find themselves entering a whole new world of excitement and adventure. When this door is open, we enter his kingdom. Better yet, his kingdom enters us.

Jesus is the door. Jesus is the host. Living, loving, and leaving what Jesus left behind means I move outside the comfort of my Dixie cups and sweet tea potlucks and into the dangers of the highways and byways. Learning to party with sinners may be in order if we really are committed to leaving what Jesus left behind. Let the party begin!

DAY 21: FINDING THE JESUS WAY

1. Who are the marginalized people in your life?
2. How can we extend hospitality toward them in a way that brings them to the party?
3. What does it look like for you to be the eccentric host?

Thoughts, Prayers, and Doodles on the Jesus Way

_____

_____

_____

_____

_____

_____

_____

_____

_____

_____

_____

_____

_____

_____

_____

CHAPTER 22

Temple . . . It's Time to Turn over a Few Tables

"You have heard that it was said . . . But I tell you that . . ."
—Matthew 5:21–22, 27–28, 31–32, 33–34, 38–39

Toxic Religion: The church is for members only.

The Jesus Way: The church is a body from which God extends his love to all people.

In the church where I serve as a pastor, we leaders are committed to changing the way people think about church so that we might change the way they think about Jesus. As a community of followers we are learning this involves deprogramming. Jesus tells us we are the body of Christ, and, as the body, we work best when we work together for his mission. This is why Jesus prayed that we might be one, in order that the world might come to know him (see John 17:21). It is a beautiful thing when the body comes together, united in his common cause.

It is our responsibility as followers to remove every possible barrier from those who are coming to Jesus. When we live, love, and leave, these barriers are removed and those who are far from God find their way to him. In Scripture there is only one barrier that must remain, and that is the barrier of Jesus on the cross. On the cross we see redemptive love at its fullest and best, and it is at the cross that all men are drawn toward the Jesus way.

The Church as the Barrier

Too often, the church becomes a barrier. That's exactly what Dave Kinnaman and Gabe Lyons demonstrated in their book *unChristian*. They asked the most unreached generation in modern history (young people age sixteen to twenty-six) what they thought of Christians, and these people had some pretty harsh words for the church. Some of the chapter titles in their book tell the story of what these people think of Christians: Hypocritical, Antihomosexual, Sheltered, Too Political, Judgmental.[8] How's that for a wake-up call? We must deprogram if we are going to remove these perceptions and the barriers they build that keep people from Jesus and his church.

Michael Frost and Alan Hirsch give us an excellent reminder of what the church is in their book *ReJesus*: "The church as the New Testament defines it is not a religious institution but rather a dynamic community of believers who participate in the way of Jesus and his work in this world."[9] All that is required, as Jesus said, is for two or three to come together in his name, and he will be there with them (Matt.18:20). God did not intend for the church to exist for itself, nor for it to be about membership. The church is not an organization to join or a country club to participate in. It is two or more followers of Jesus gathered together in his name to live out his ways and accomplish his purposes. We must also realize the church does not exist primarily for those who are already followers of Jesus. According to Jesus we are the "salt of the earth" (Matt. 5:13) and the "light of the world" (v. 14), representing Jesus to the nations.

This is where deprogramming comes in. Jesus explained the need for deprogramming when he said, "No one pours new wine into old wineskins. If he does, the new wine will burst the skins, the wine will run out and the wineskins will be ruined" (Luke 5:37). Jesus is the Messiah bringing new wine, but the religious still want the old ways. When new wine was poured into old wineskins, the wine fermented, expanded the wineskin, and the wineskin burst. Jesus is teaching his followers that wine is intended to shape the wineskin, not the other way around. He is telling us that God is doing a new thing, and he is that new thing. He goes on to tell them that this new thing can't exist within the context of old religious forms and structures. New wine requires new skins. It is only when you put new wine in a new wineskin that the wine can have complete freedom in expanding and shaping the skin. We often begin with the container instead of the creator of the container, spending all of our time focused on the skin (the church), instead of the wine (Jesus).

This results in creating institutional expressions of church that keep people at an arm's length from God. Yet when you begin with Jesus, all the rules change. Throughout the Gospels, Jesus constantly moved toward people who were far from God, teaching them and bringing them in to himself. Church buildings sit still. Church bodies move toward people.

Flipping a Few Tables

There's an incident in the life of Jesus that stands out to me— the time Jesus entered the temple area and began driving out those who were buying and selling there, overturning tables and benches (see Mark 11:15–18). At first glance it appears that Jesus was angry because they were buying and selling, but on a closer look it has more to do with *where* they were buying and selling. Many of the worshippers came from miles around, and it was customary for vendors to sell small animals for sacrificing just outside the temple. However, in this particular encounter, these transactions were taking place inside the court of the temple—the one place all people could come and worship, Jew and Gentile alike. Jesus' outburst was the result of barriers placed by religious leaders that prevented the people from worshipping.

People far from God need a safe place to experience Jesus and his ways. What better place for them to experience Jesus than among his people, gathered together to fulfill his mission? When we realize that we are the body of Christ and that God makes his appeal through us, it changes everything. The people of God ought to be the most accepting, forgiving, and loving people on the earth. In other words, we ought to be like Jesus, for he lives in us and loves through us.

What if collectively we become a safe place where people far from God could live among us as they explore, experience, and experiment with the Jesus way? They are our friends and we must welcome them into our lives and treat them as such. We can't afford to move on without them—the mission of God is at stake. Those who are far from God are at stake. Becoming a friend to sinners is messy business, but cleaning up new wine that burst old wineskins is even messier.

Redefining Church

Lately I have been pondering a series of questions centered on the definition of the church. There are many competing definitions of the church. Since this book is primarily about the gospel and Jesus and his ways, I have been asking myself, "What is Jesus' definition of church?" If I'm completely honest with you, I don't have the answer. However, I'm not satisfied with a definition that is more about an organization or an institution. The other thing I find interesting is that Jesus never laid out a clear definition of the church. I am convinced that any definition of church should be centered on the fact that, as the church, we are first and foremost the body of Christ. Our mission is clear. The things Jesus began to teach and do, he continues through his people. This is exactly what Luke had to say, "In my former book, Theophilus, I wrote about all that Jesus began to do and to teach until the day he was taken up to heaven, after giving instructions through the Holy Spirit to the apostles he had chosen" (Acts 1:1–2). What Jesus began, he continues through his church.

When we consider what it means to be the church through the lens of the gospel, we are confronted with the fact that it is possible to be part of the organized church and miss Jesus altogether. I am not opposed to the organized church, but I do believe passionately that the church as we know it is in need of reformation. That's why I do feel a sense of calling. That calling is to be a missionary to the church. It is the organized church as we know it that has the greatest potential for being the church.

Last Thoughts on the Church

There are those who have given up on the church as an organization. I have not. There is something potent when followers of Jesus come together to celebrate their King on a regular basis with the freedom to open the door and invite those far from God to join them. This door should flow both ways. Because people far from God need time, a place, and people to help them navigate the journey, the church can serve as a vital partner in our missional enterprise. At the same time, we must be quick to allow our understanding, experience, and relationship with Jesus to shape the form, expression, and mission of the church—not the other way around.

Every week we have hundreds of people attend our church who are far from God. Every week some of them are choosing to join Jesus. The organized church can be a powerful force when it sees its surrounding community as a mission field and sees itself as the missionary. When this happens, we make great strides toward being the church. As God sent Jesus, he sends his people, and together in community he sends his church. However, we must never forget that as his people we are the church, and apart from his Spirit and people, all you have is bricks and mortar.

DAY 22: FINDING THE JESUS WAY

1. What are some of the attitudes and perceptions that keep people far from God?
2. What is your definition of the church?
3. What are some ways we can reprogram or deprogram the organized church?
4. If the church really is a living organism, what are some implications for the organized church?

Thoughts, Prayers, and Doodles on the Jesus Way

Oneness . . . That's How We Roll

*"May they be brought to complete unity to let the
world know that you sent me and have loved them
even as you have loved me."*

—John 17:23

> **Toxic Religion:** My religion is about me.
>
> **The Jesus Way:** The church is one body and we
> are all part of it.

I was in a Middle Eastern desert watching men drag a buffalo across
the courtyard. The animal sensed what was happening. He dug his
hoofed feet into the hard earth. When I saw the crescent shaped
knife, I felt uneasy, but this whole situation made me think of Jesus
in some strange way, like a lamb headed to slaughter.

I thought of Jesus, before he began his ordeal and ultimately the
evening he spent with his disciples at the Mount of Olives. Knowing
that his life was about to end, he prayed.

"I pray also for those who will believe in me through their message, that all of them may *be one*, Father, just as you are in me and I am in you. May they also be in us so that the world may believe that you have sent me. I have given them the glory that you gave me, that they may *be one* as we *are one*: I in them and you in me. May they be brought to *complete unity* to let the world know that you sent me and have loved them even as you have loved me." (John 17:20–23, emphasis added)

Extreme Persecution

It may be hard for us followers in the Western church to understand, but in many parts of the world there is a tremendous price that comes with following Jesus. It's not news to tell you there is currently a significant amount of persecution for those who follow Jesus in places like the Middle East. In one of the cities I often visit, your identification card is stamped with the word "Christian" if you claim to be a Christian. If your card is so marked, you don't want to be stopped on a lonely road. In a more extreme place where I am involved, Christianity will land you in jail or cost you your life. There you will find moral police and moral judges to deal with those who might follow Jesus and his ways. In this country, if you are a follower of Jesus, it is considered apostasy. Apostasy often carries a death sentence.

I've recently met a number of new friends from these hostile places. Two of them lost their fathers to martyrdom. I earlier told the story of the young woman whose child was taken from her. She hasn't seen her daughter in five years, since the girl was four. She was even given an option by the moral judge: deny Jesus and she could be reunited with her daughter. She refused to deny Jesus, thus the five years of separation. Even as I type these words, two other young women have been put in prison for apostasy. In one appearance before a very agitated judge, he promised one of the women death. Her only reply was, "Whatever you must do, do it quickly." At this time they are still awaiting their trial. These are our brothers and sisters.

Back to My Buffalo Story

I was in the Middle East with a small group of pastors and leaders conducting leadership training for pastors from all over their country, and at this conference one guest stood out to me. He was the head of the evangelical churches in that part of the world. He was an elderly man who spoke softly and wore a priest's collar under his suit jacket. He spoke with a boldness that belied his age, challenging the weak church to abandon the safety nets of its church buildings and permits to meet, and go into the world, risking followers' lives for the sake of the gospel.

I was asked to speak at this event about intentionally stepping out of our comfort zones, yet this church leader spoke in ways

I could not as he demonstrated it with his life. This man has found God's favor, and I am certain he will be a key to the kingdom coming to this region of the world. As I listened to him talk about his experiences, challenging the church toward boldness, I found myself fearing for his life, yet he didn't seem to share the fear.

Playing It Safe and Taking Risk

There are two types of churches in this region: those licensed by the government and those considered illegal that meet in homes. Many of the leaders at this particular conference were pastors of churches licensed by the government (one of the ways the government keeps tabs on the church). A few of them are risking their lives by starting underground or house churches. For many of them, having a license to operate limits their willingness to risk losing their ability to operate. This translates to "mind your own business by doing church for card-carrying Christians, but leave the Great Commission to the underground church."

This conference was a step in shaking that up. Historically the Middle Eastern church has been hindered by its isolation from other followers of Jesus and other churches. There are many denominations in that part of the country. Each of them feels it is right, almost to the point of believing that its way is the only way to heaven. Sadly, this should sound familiar to the overly religious. We don't seem to see that infighting and disagreements only serve to divide believers rather than unite them, weakening the effectiveness of the church. We have come to believe that our rites and rituals and practices will make us strong, forgetting Jesus' prayer in the garden.

Oneness Leads to Boldness

This is what Jesus was praying for when he prayed that we might be one. The church is anemic when it is scattered and isolated, but when the church comes together to make a statement, it is loud. When the church comes together to live out the love of Jesus, it is deafening. Satan knows what he is doing by attempting to keep the church divided.

I saw the importance of our oneness through a new lens during that meeting in the Middle East, as the pastors' conference reminded me of the American civil rights movement. Peace did not prevail in that movement until a young pastor named Martin Luther King Jr. was used by God to call people together. Under his leadership people rose up, united, and fought the forces of evil that held many in oppression. Imagine what might have happened had the church as a whole stood united in opposition to discrimination.

The church is a mighty force; Jesus told Peter that the gates of hell would not stand against it (see Matt. 16:18). When we stand together under God for the right reason, we cannot be defeated. In churches outside the U.S., those who follow Jesus may represent only a small minority of people, and we must stand with them in unity if they are to survive. We should take our direction from the believers who gathered in prayer with Peter and John. As they prayed together, their meeting room was shaken. They were filled with the Holy Spirit and began to speak with boldness (see Acts 4:23–31).

If we are to witness the work of God in the church today, we must put away our divisions and petty religion in favor of bringing the church together. There is only one banner under which we can all fit—Jesus—and there's room for all of us. God is moving in the Middle East, in the United States, in China, in Africa, in South America, and it is our responsibility to aid the church in coming together for the advancement of the movement. Jesus' revolution is underway. Unlike other movements, it is a peaceful movement. It is filled with different kinds of warriors. These warriors are ordinary people from all over the world committed to the way of Jesus, the way of peace on Earth. They are peacemakers.

We Are Not Exempt

A few years back I worked for a large denomination. We launched an initiative to train up a new generation of pastors for the purpose of planting churches all across North America. From my perspective this was a very important initiative, because God is reseeding North America with churches that are passionate about Jesus and his ways. This movement is saying no to religion and the things that divide us, and yes to a new kind of Christianity; a Christianity defined by a global commitment to the Jesus way.

This initiative required the partnering of several agencies, schools, and organizations. It was my responsibility to bring these groups together for greater impact. What I underestimated was the amount of division and relational brokenness among these groups. It became obvious early that we did not know each other, and there was very little trust within the body.

I set up seven meetings across our nation and Canada for the purpose of bringing these groups together. Each meeting was well attended and took place over two days. The dynamics of these meetings were very predictable. The first day consisted of my unpacking our strategy and answering their questions and concerns. These were hard meetings where tempers often flared. In one of the meetings a leader came to me during a break and apologized for being so angry and informed me he was leaving. I agreed with him that for the sake of the whole that would be best. My heart was broken. During these meeting we had many breakthroughs. However, none of them were easy.

As I reflected on these meetings, it became apparent to me that the Enemy was having a field day. As I thought about it, if I were the Enemy, I, too, would seek to divide us. Jesus understood this when he prayed that we might be one. When we come together, there is no stopping the church as a mighty life- and culture-changing force. When we come together, his kingdom comes on Earth as it is in heaven. When we are divided by fable, opinions, power structures, sin, and preference, we are already defeated.

It's Time to Come Together

As a pastor, I am more convicted than ever to ensure that our churches are united with all of God's people. Our church has instituted a church-planting residency program for those who feel called of God to plant new churches. The beautiful part is that last year we helped plant a Baptist Church and a Free Methodist Church, and this year we are helping plant a Presbyterian Church, in Australia of all places! We are committed to planting churches, not by denomination, but by the belief that Jesus is the one and only way, and that the church is designed to reach people who are far from God.

When Jesus invites us into a relationship with him, he brings his entire family, the whole messy lot. We are the church, and we are brothers and sisters. We are one, and we must continually pray for oneness and for boldness if our world is to be won. At the same time, it must not stop there. We must reach across the aisle. We must reach across the city. We must reach across the oceans. We must reach across our petty differences. After all, we are the church. We are brothers and sisters. Again, I pray, Jesus, show us your way. Amen.

DAY 23: FINDING THE JESUS WAY

1. Why is it important that we come together as one church?
2. How does religion keep the church apart?
3. What can we learn from the churches in the Middle East?
4. What religious attitudes keep us from becoming one?

Thoughts, Prayers, and Doodles on the Jesus Way

Closing Thoughts

As I come to the end of this book, I am once again reminded that the Jesus way is a lifelong journey of following him. He invites us into his life, a life filled with bold adventures characterized by our becoming less and less and him becoming more and more. Since this book has been about the gospel, I am struck by the words of John in the closing verse of the Gospels, "Jesus did many other things as well. If every one of them were written down, I suppose that even the whole world would not have room for the books that would be written" (John 21:25). This verse is a reminder that there is so much more to Jesus and his ways than I could ever write about. My ramblings and musings don't even begin to scratch the surface of what living the Jesus ways entails for me or for us collectively. My story is only a small part of his story. My prayer is that my story might serve as a catalyst in your journey for losing your religion and discovering or rediscovering the simplicity of Jesus and his ways.

For me it has served this purpose. Now more than ever, I have a hunger for finding the Jesus way. Every day as I start a fresh adventure, there is a new hunger to see Jesus more clearly. The prayer I introduced to you early on in this writing still dominates my prayer life, *Jesus, show me your way.* Each new revelation about him leads me to the threshold of another. Each day as I reflect on his teaching and his life, I find new hope, purpose, and meaning. I can't wait to see what he has in store for me as I approach another day in eternity. This is my prayer for all of us as we come to embrace him and his ways—and as we live like him, love like him, and leave what he left behind.

May God's peace be with you now and forever!

Notes

1. See http://en.wikipedia.org/wiki/Herodians.
2. Francis Chan, *Crazy Love* (Colorado Springs, CO: David Cook, 2009).
3. See www.stanford.edu/group/King/publications/sermons/ 571117.002_Loving_Your_Enemies.html.
4. See www.mkgandhi.org/articles/true_visionary.htm.
5. C. S. Lewis, *The Chronicles of Narnia: The Lion, the Witch, and the Wardrobe.* 1950, C. S. Lewis Pte., Ltd.
6. Rick Warren, *The Purpose Driven Life* (Grand Rapids, MI: Zondervan, 2002), 17.
7. Frederick Buechner, *Telling the Truth* (New York, NY: Harper & Row, 1977), 66.
8. David Kinnaman and Gabe Lyons, *unChristian* (Grand Rapids, MI: Baker Books, 2008), 34.
9. Michael Frost and Alan Hirsch, *ReJesus* (Sydney: Strand Publishing, 2009), 29.